Doris Kartinyeri lives in a small house in Adelaide with her fifteen-year-old dog, Sharah. When she's not speaking on the Stolen Generations to groups and schools, or involved with the Enfield Outreach program, Doris likes to crochet or work in her garden. Visits from her three children and thirteen grand-children keep her on her toes.

Doris has just completed three children's books and is now working on another book.

KICK THE TIN

By
Doris E. Kartinyeri

Spinifex Press Pty Ltd
504 Queensberry Street
North Melbourne, Vic. 3051
Australia
women@spinifexpress.com.au
www.spinifexpress.com.au

First published by Spinifex Press, 2000
Second edition 2002
Copyright © Doris E. Kartinyeri, 2000
Copyright © on page layout and design: Spinifex Press, 2000

Cover design by Deb Snibson
Edited by Miriel Lenore and Kath Knapsey
Typeset in Plantin by Palmer Higgs
Made and printed in Australia by McPherson's Printing Group

National Library of Australia
Cataloguing-in-Publication data:
Kartinyeri, Doris
Kick the Tin
ISBN 1875559 95 7
1. Kartinyeri, Doris. 2. Aborigines, Australian – South
Australia – Child welfare. 3. Aborigines, Australian –
Biography. 4. Aborigines, Australian – South Australia –
Children – Government policy. 5. Aborigines, Australian –
South Australia – Treatment – History. I. Title.
305.89915

This publication is assisted by the Australia Council,
the Australian Government's arts funding and
advisory body.
The publication of this work was supported by the
Government of South Australia through Arts SA.

ARTSA

CONTENTS

Acknowledgments   ix
Preface   xiii
Foreword   xvii
Glossary   xx

STOLEN   5

PROTECTION   13

THE BEGINNING OF GRIEF   29

SHUNTED ABOUT   57

NEED TO BELONG   69

JOURNEY FROM REALITY   81
    The Great Gardens of Monato   81
    Broken Spirit   92
    Oh, What a Feeling!   99

MY GUIDING HANDS   105
    Connections   120

FINDING MY VOICE   123

NGARRINDJERI MIMINI   135

Warning: Some of the people mentioned in this book have passed away. I tell their stories with the deepest respect.

I dedicate this book

to

my children

Jennadene Packham, John Packham,

Tanya Thompson and

to

my grandchildren

Jamie, Rick, Bradley, Keiden, Tamara, Chantelle,

Verlaine, Kirsty, Jacob, Colin, Rhys (deceased),

Jade, Paige and Bella

We are the stolen children

Who were taken away

Torn from our mothers' breasts

What can a child do?

Where can a child turn?

Where is the guiding hand

A child is meant to have?

ACKNOWLEDGMENTS

My early childhood was shared with many brothers and sisters at Colebrook Home. This book is for them. For the living and the deceased. Many years shared with imagination, laughter and tears. The memories will always be with me. I thank the people who contributed their stories to this book.

The love and encouragement of my children and grandchildren have been the source of strength which has enabled me to complete this book. My children have always stood by me and given me the incentive to go on. The main purpose in writing this book is to record the story of my life for them.

I want to show my appreciation to Dr. Doreen Kartinyeri, my older sister, for her assistance with information concerning my family. Reconnecting with Doreen was the beginning of my journey. Her tireless campaign for Aboriginal rights is indicative of her spirit. Doreen's involvement with Aboriginal Communities in South Australia, her publications and her

Aboriginal genealogy work with the Adelaide Museum have inspired me.

Throughout my life there are many friends who have inspired and strengthened me to go on. One particular friend, Janet Hannah Tooby, has given me strength by just being a friend. Her gentleness and free spirit have enriched me.

My close contact with Auntie Faith Thomas from Quorn Colebrook Home has had a big impact. We shared our stories of Colebrook. The long hours and many phone calls allowed me to include the wonderful story behind the Colebrook Tree. I want to thank Auntie Faith for her knowledge and interest. Thanks for the many hours of laughter.

Another dear friend is Ellen Rowley who has been a tremendous help and inspiration with her expertise and her ideas. The stories that we shared helped us both through our illnesses.

Zora Wenham, an English/drama teacher, helped me with her concern and encouragement through my tears and mood swings while writing this book. I attended Torrens Valley College at Gilles Plains for a few years as a student doing an English literacy course. Thanks to Una and Don Strempel who gave me support from the start.

I want to show my appreciation to editor, Miriel Lenore, for her dedication throughout my struggles to complete this book. Thanks for your tolerance. Thanks also to Ruth Raintree for her assistance and her strength.

Thanks to Arts SA, the South Australian Department for the Arts, for their support in funding me as a writer. Many thanks to Heather Shearer (Kemarre) who has shown tremendous interest in my work and been supportive in every way.

Lastly, I would like to thank Susan Hawthorne, Kath Knapsey and all the staff at Spinifex Press for publishing *Kick the Tin* and sharing many jokes along the way.

Lorraine Smith and Doris Kartinyeri.

PREFACE
BY DOREEN KARTINYERI

I was ten when my sister Doris Eileen Kartinyeri was born at the Raukkan Community Hospital, 8 September 1945. After Mum had Doris, she was very sick, so she and Doris were moved to the bigger hospital at Murray Bridge. Dad went to Murray Bridge so he could be with them. Mum died just one month after Doris was born.

When Dad came home to organise Mum's funeral we thought he'd be bringing home our new sister. But Dad said the doctor wanted to keep the baby in hospital until after the funeral.

The day after the funeral, Dad and his sister, Auntie Martha, went back to the hospital to pick up baby Doris. When they got there, they found out that the welfare officer from the Protector's office, Sister McKenzie, had taken Doris the day before the funeral. The entire family was devastated. I remember my Grandmother Sally screaming and crying for Doris. Oscar and I sat with the youngest two, Connie who was three years old and Ron, who was five, and we all cried together.

My cousin Florence Rankine moved into our house with our grandparents Archie and Sally Kartinyeri to help Dad look after us. As I was only ten years old I was unable to care for my family. The welfare officer was by then thinking of taking the rest of the children.

For a long time our home was full of tears. Connie and Ronnie were missing Mum and cried themselves to sleep every night. Grandmother Sally cried whenever she thought of Doris and kept asking where Doris could be. Was she alright? Our cousin Florence, known to us as sister Flo, was a big help to Dad, Minoo, Nana and me.

It took Sister McKenzie over three months to catch me. At first we had a system with the bus driver. When Sister McKenzie was on the bus, the driver beeped the horn at the corner to warn me to hide. I'd grab something to eat, a potato and an onion, and race down to the prickly pear patch at the back of our place and stay away all night until I was sure she was gone. Eventually Grandmother Sally talked to me and told me that I should go with Sister McKenzie so that I could be with my baby sister, Doris. She thought I would also be with my three cousins who Mum had looked after when her brother Ron went to the

Riverland to work. Our cousins had been taken when Mum got sick the year before.

On my way to Adelaide I was so happy. I would see Doris at last. I was also excited that I was going to see Thelma, Lila and Elsie who were like my sisters. But when I arrived at the home, only Elsie was there. Thelma and Lila had been placed in the Queen Victoria Hospital as domestic help. Doris was not there. I was so hurt I couldn't eat and wouldn't do anything the matron asked. I had just turned eleven and could not understand what was going on.

Months later I still didn't know where Doris was. One day we all had to go to the Protector's office to get measured for our winter clothes. I knew Sister McKenzie would be there taking everyone's measurements. As I walked there with some of the other girls from Fullarton, I decided to try and force Sister McKenzie to tell me where Doris was. I rushed over to the War Memorial and started to climb it. I got really high up and was starting to get scared when I yelled out to the other girls to go and tell Sister McKenzie I was going to jump if she didn't tell me where Doris was. She came pretty quick, but she still didn't want to tell me. So I wouldn't come down until she gave in and told me Doris was at Colebrook. They had separated us by putting me in the Fullarton Home and Doris in Colebrook.

One of the girls who was there at the War Memorial also had sisters at Colebrook, so when we could, the two of us went on the train to visit. Dad, Oscar and my cousin Nelson visited Doris at Colebrook too, although they weren't able to take her home. But Grandmother Sally and Grandfather Archie never met Doris. They died before Doris got out of Colebrook.

Only those who have been taken from their families can know what Doris has been through in her life.

For all those who did not make it back to their loved ones, their families and homes, and missed out on knowing their language, culture, tradition, and identity, **we say sorry**.

But for those who, like Doris, have survived, we say God Bless and good luck.

Dr Doreen Kartinyeri
26-7-2000

FOREWORD

BY LOWITJA O'DONOGHUE

Kick the Tin is the story of one woman's journey. It is a painful passage which progresses from beautiful childhood innocence with all its mischief, curiosity and laughter, to a terrifying world where sexual abuse, confusion and alienation are a backdrop to an emerging adolescence.

Doris' powerful writing evokes characters and places so vividly that we are with her every step along her road to the edge of insanity and back again. It is a story of courage and survival, powerfully demonstrating how the human spirit can soar despite all the injuries and injustices which threaten to drag it down.

I am sure that every reader will be moved and will understand more about the Stolen Generations by reading this account of Doris' life and her experiences as a tjitji tjuta—a Colebrook kid.

It is difficult to explain the emotions and memories that this book has stirred in me, for not only was I a Colebrook kid as well, but also, I had some responsibility for Doris—she was one of my Colebrook babies.

The older kids (I was thirteen) looked after the little ones who were known as 'our special babies'. For three years before I left Colebrook, Doris was my special baby. I remember her lovely smile and beautiful curly hair, and I remember many of the scenes and people that she describes in her Colebrook story. I have wept at these memories. To think that I was not there for her in her most lonely and frightened times, brings with it an indescribable pain.

And so, as well as commending this book to readers everywhere—which I wholeheartedly do—I would also like to express a personal and deeply felt message for Doris.

Doris, thank you for this wonderful book. It is testimony to a strong, creative and loving spirit. It offers strength to indigenous people all over Australia who continue in their struggle to come to terms with what it means to be a part of the Stolen Generations.

I know that writing this book has been a huge milestone in your own journey of healing, and I celebrate with you this extraordinary achievement. I hope this is just a first instalment and that you will use your wonderful talent with words for many more projects.

For not being there in the hour of your need, I can only say I'm sorry. I just wish I had known what was happening.

GLOSSARY

cutta: silly
kungka: woman
maku: witchetty grub
mana: buttocks, bottom
maru: black, Aboriginal
mimini: woman
ngunti: lie
nukkin: looking
nunga: Aboriginal person
palya: good
pilyki: dirty
pungyn: greedy
tjilpi: old man
tjina: feet
tjina nikiti: barefoot
tjitji tjuta: children
tjuni pulka: fat
wama: alcohol
wurengi pulgi: nut house

I wouldn't have attempted this book had it not been for my daughter, Jennadene. She was sitting with me one time while I was in hospital. We were talking away together.

'I am going to write a book!' I heard myself say.

'Mum, you do that,' she replied in a soft voice.

I have an illness. It has taken me a long time to come to terms with it. My healing began when I decided to write my autobiography and I continued to write throughout my illnesses. With lots of coffee, cigarettes and frustration, with laughter and medication, the journey began. In and out of mental institutions I managed to complete this book.

I recall my stay at this *wurengi pulgi*[1]. I had a brilliant inspiration. In a flash I knew what I was going to call this book. Yes, *Kick the Tin*.

---

1 wurengi pulgi: nut house

'Kick the Tin' was a game we played as children at Colebrook Home. The idea of the game was that we all had to stand around the tin. One person, 'It', stood next to the tin. Then someone would run in and give one hell of a kick to the tin and all us *maru*[2] kids would run for our lives, scattering to hide. 'It' would run and fetch the tin and place one foot on it, look around, then start searching for the kids. The idea of the game was for 'It' to tag the kids found and for the others to make it back to the tin without being caught.

My life has been literally kicked about, just like the tin we used to kick around. I believe that our Aboriginal brothers and sisters experienced much suffering because of the abusive behaviour of white fella governments and regimental, oppressive institutions. By running and hiding we escaped white fellas' way. To numb our pain we drank alcohol excessively; abusing our bodies in violent relationships, crushing our spirits, repeating the violent relationships of our protectors. This cycle of suffering continues. Everybody has now scattered in their own directions following their dreams and discovering their roots, taking different avenues just as in the game, 'Kick the Tin'.

---

2 maru: black, Aboriginal

2

IT'S JUST THE BEGINNING

Mother you have carried me for nine wonderful
months
you have fed me with love
you feel my kicks and movements which please you
this bond is shared by two

protected from all pain, hate and cruelty
I move with contentment inside you
as you sing with laughter
a bond that can never be broken

my movements tell you that it is time
for a new beginning
my time has come to endure my new life
my birth brings you pain

we shared our lives together
for such a short time

STOLEN

The day I was conceived, life began. The nurturing began. I was surrounded by love, protected in my mother's womb. A sense of bonding was all around.

Back row (L–R): Nancy who died before Doris was born, Thelma Kartinyeri, Connie Kartinyeri (Baby), Doreen Kartinyeri. Front row: Ronald Kartinyeri (Squashy).

The event of my birth started life shattering experiences for me and for my family. I was born 8 September 1945 at Raukkan, a Ngarrindjeri community at Point McLeay on the shores of Lake Alexandrina. My mother died of complications in Murray Bridge Hospital on October 8, just one month after my birth. Within a few days of the death of my mother, I was stolen from my family. Welfare officers from the Aboriginal Protection Board removed me from the Murray Bridge Hospital and placed me in Colebrook Home without my father knowing.

I stayed at Colebrook Home until I turned fourteen years old. I was never told that I was removed from my family. I was never told that my mother had died. In all of my childhood, I was never taken back to my family.

About four years ago, I went to meet with my older sister, Doreen, at our friend's place to learn about my family. We sat in the confined space of Margaret's kitchen. Doreen has written numerous books tracing our family tree. She has helped me to understand more about my heritage, a heritage rightly mine from birth, which was taken away from me.

First I learned of the disturbing facts surrounding our family at the time of my birth. Doreen told me gently that there were complications when Mum gave birth to me at Raukkan. A few days later the nursing sister at Raukkan called on the Aboriginal mid-wife, Mrs. Beatrice Karpany. She asked Beatrice to come down and see Mum as she was running an intensely high temperature. Beatrice argued with the sister to take my mother to Murray Bridge Hospital. My mother and I were taken to the hospital at Murray Bridge where we stayed; Mum getting treatment until she died 8 October 1945. That was on the Eight Hours Day public holiday, which was what they used as Labour Day.

It was decided by the family that Mum's funeral would be at Raukkan on Friday the 12th of October.

Doreen was finding it hard, in that kitchen, to tell me about the events that followed. I waited in silence. Still it was difficult for Doreen to speak. In an angry voice she told me that our Mum's body was transported all the way from Murray Bridge to Raukkan on the back of a ute. We sat in disbelief, in a frozen state. My eyes filled with tears. Doreen continued to speak in an awkward and quivering voice, jotting down notes for me. She told me that on the day after my Mother's funeral, on the Saturday, my Dad went back to

Murray Bridge Hospital to collect me. When he arrived with my Auntie Martha to pick me up from the hospital, I was gone. He was told that Sister McKenzie had removed me from the hospital and taken me to Adelaide on the day before my Mum's funeral. This must have been extremely devastating for my father, particularly while he was still in mourning over the death of his wife.

The family had gathered when Dad came home without me. The whole family was traumatised to hear that I was not coming home. Auntie Martha was soon telling everyone that I was taken. Doreen ran down to Auntie Phillis very upset. No one could understand why no phone message came from the Protector to say Doris was taken. All my family had offered to look after me.

Doreen told me that Dad went back to Tailem Bend to get another train to take him to Adelaide to see where I was placed. He went to see a Mr. Penhall at the Protection Board in Kintore Avenue, Adelaide. Dad was greatly upset and he cursed and argued with Mr. Penhall, as he wanted to know where I was. Dad was informed that I was in a home and that it was better for me to be with other Aboriginal children in a home. Dad's reply to this was, 'What the fuck would you know about what is best for my daughter, or that she is better off with other Aboriginal children. She has her own family. Her nanna would look after her as well as you would. Or better!'

Mr. Penhall talked to Dad and tried to convince him that I should stay at the home until I was old enough for Nanna to look after me. But Dad never agreed. On 9 January 1946, my father signed a document giving me into the care of Colebrook Home until I reached sixteen. He thought he was signing the form for child endowment.

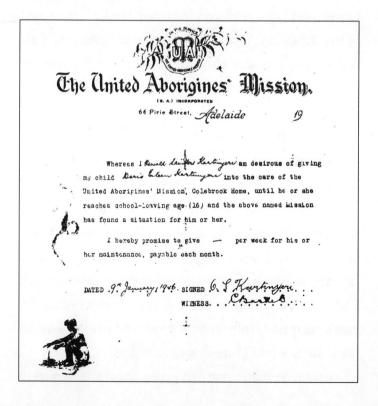

The United Aborigines' Mission.
(S. A.) INCORPORATED
66 Pirie Street, Adelaide   19

Whereas I *Rewell Sanifer Kartinyeri* am desirous of giving my child *Doris Eileen Kartinyeri* into the care of the United Aborigines' Mission, Colebrook Home, until he or she reaches school-leaving age (16) and the above named Mission has found a situation for him or her.

I hereby promise to give — per week for his or her maintenance, payable each month.

DATED 9ᵗ January, 1946. SIGNED *O. S. Kartinyeri*
WITNESS. . . . *Charles* . . . . .

It was an unnatural act for any Aboriginal child to be separated from their family. I didn't receive any parental nurturing or have the privilege of growing up with my brothers and sisters. I never experienced any emotions involving the loss of my mother. I lost my family ties and heritage. I know this has affected my whole family.

My eldest sister Doreen was just ten years old, living at Raukkan and making feather flowers to support the family. After the death of our mother, Doreen was also removed from our family and placed in the Salvation Army Girl's Home at Fullarton. This meant that she was also separated from me and my family. This was a traumatic time for Dad and our grandparents, Archie and Sally Kartinyeri.

It was obvious to our family that the Government deliberately wanted to separate us and did not want us together. My sister Connie, who was three years old when I was taken, stayed on at Raukkan with our brothers, Oscar and Ronald, and our grandparents. Oscar worked with Dad on the mission. Grand-mother Sally cried every day for me. She wondered if I had curls and looked like Connie who had beautiful black curly hair. It brought sorrow and pain as I heard these stories that Doreen had to tell me.

It's taken many years to get to know the surviving

members of my family. Both of my parents were from Point McLeay, known as Raukkan. They were both Ngarrindjeri. Oswald Saunders Kartinyeri and Thelma Christabel Kartinyeri (née Rigney) were living at the Mission when I was born. My father was born 26 December 1908 and died 9 July 1979. He was 71 years old when he passed away. My mother was born 8 November 1910 and died in 1945 at the age of 35.

My mother was a very strong and loving woman. She took great pride in my family's small cottage set by the lake. Oscar often sat on the bed while my mother unpicked dresses and skirts. She unpicked old jumpers and made clothes for the less fortunate children. My mother was very artistic in keeping her house neat and tidy. She kept herself busy sewing and making feather flowers and mats from rushes. She was a good cook. There were seven children in our family— five girls and two boys. Oscar was the eldest of the family followed by Doreen and Ronald. Then Connie and me. Nancy and Alma both died before I was born.

Colebrook provided me with an extended family of other Aboriginal children who had also been removed from their families. Life as a child in the home was enjoyable up to a point, however we were deprived of family affection.

I understand why there is a lot of hatred in the Aboriginal community where children have been forcibly removed from their families by white governments. How could anyone think that apologies or money could make up for the lost years and the terrible trauma and emotional damage caused to my family?

PROTECTION

*'Colebrook started with Sister R Hyde and Sister
D Rutter. They were Colebrook. What we had was
constant love and attention ...'*
                                    Auntie Faith Thomas

Colebrook originated at the United Aboriginal
Mission at Oodnadatta in the year of 1924. By 1926,
there was a small house with Sister Hyde in charge.
The government policy at that time was to remove
half-caste children from their traditional culture and
family and to assimilate them into white society. The
original home accommodated only five children taken
from their families. Soon there were twelve. In May
of 1927 a small house on the outskirts of Quorn
was rented and when it became too small, another was
purchased. It was officially named Colebrook Home
after a UAM President and remained there in Quorn
for sixteen years, by which time conditions had
become quite overcrowded. In 1943 a third home was
established at Eden Hills for the children and was
renamed Colebrook Training Centre.

The Eden Hills Colebrook was a huge and beautiful
looking building with a verandah surrounding the

sides and front, supported by rows of great posts. It stood on acres of land with beautiful gardens and tall gum trees. The front steps led to the entrance of the main office and the common room. It had a huge cellar. The girls' dormitories faced the main drive. The centre courtyard separated the boys quarters from the girls quarters. The courtyard was the centre point for a lot of happenings.

This building was home for many *maru* kids like myself. We were the stolen children who, for some reason, were taken away from our biological Aboriginal parents and heritage and placed in Colebrook Home. Between 1943 and 1972 some three hundred and fifty Aboriginal children passed through Colebrook Home. This was our home and we respected it. We were happy in our own way, laughing, crying, and just being an extended family with a lot of love.

The children who came to the home were from near and far, north, south, east and west, so we developed a lingo that was taught to us by the older ones. It was Ngarrindjeri, Pitjantjatjara, English and some of our own words all mixed up together. Some of our *maru* words are used throughout the book.

I felt secure with my many brothers and sisters. I recall two older boys arriving: Yami who was blind and a much older lad Monty, who carried their only possessions, their swags. They had both come down from the north. Monty was a tall, sleek, full-blooded Aboriginal who wore cowboy boots. He made quite an impression.

The older girls sometimes had responsibility to look after their 'special babies'. We called them Auntie. My Colebrook sister, Avis, was cared for by Auntie Amy O'Donoghue. And Auntie Lois O'Donoghue, now Dr Lowitja O'Donoghue, cared for me.

Most of the Colebrook kids had nicknames. Some of the nicknames that were given to the kids really suited them. I was called Canary, as I always seemed to be whistling about the place. I remember one of the boys, Graham McKenzie, whom we used to call Spider Legs. He was always carving. He carved an Aboriginal face from a rock that he had found in the cliffs. I thought he was so clever. I remember we all gathered around him as he showed off his carving. There was Jappy. She always pressed her nose against a widow pane. We thought she looked like a Jap. Alice, with her curly hair, we called Jibby because she reminded us of a sheep. There was Bulldog who resembled a bulldog and Bullock who was always chasing the boys. I could name quite a few others but I don't think it would be appreciated.

Sister Hyde and Sister Rutter were in charge at the home until 1952. The two ladies were devoted to the care of the many Aboriginal children entrusted to them. My early memories of these two wonderful women are vivid and long lasting. They both lived on faith, 'The Good Lord will provide.' They always had an abundance of love and their gentle warm smiles were always present. They did the cooking and the local ladies from the churches did the mending. Their work will always be special to me, and I think, to all those who knew them. When I close my eyes, images of them are so clear.

I can see Sister Hyde standing before me, a short middle-aged woman wearing a floral cotton dress, plain and no make-up, her silver grey hair in a bun. Her podgy build was comforting to us, as were her hugs of reassurance. Her high-heeled lace up shoes added to the matronly image. In contrast, Sister Rutter was small and thin with a frail body. The sounds of the clippity-clop of their high-heeled shoes alerted us when they were entering our dormitories. This was a comforting sound.

The appearances of these two refined missionary ladies will always be embedded in my mind. Sisters Hyde and Rutter raised me from a babe in arms till I was seven. The atmosphere these sisters created is a pleasurable memory. The sisters and the other children were my extended family. There was a great feeling of belonging and being wanted. Being in the presence of these two ladies gave me a sense of security, belonging and love that I was unable to receive from my true family.

A bell was situated in the central courtyard and a senior staff member rang the bell for each meal. Then the race was on to try and be the first in line. The girls all wore aprons and we had to hold out our hands to be checked for cleanliness as we stood in line for our meals. The whole neighbourhood must have heard the ringing of the bell and known the times of our meals. It could be heard all over Eden Hills. It rang for us to come for meals or for prayer meetings or to line up for a piece of fruit. Or to be spoilt with a small bottle of coke. This was a real treat.

I am not sure how many children were in the home at any one time but it sure seemed an awful lot to me. We always had plenty to eat, three solid meals a day. The staff took turns to cook. There were times when we had to eat bread and dripping while the staff had butter. Our meals were pretty basic with lots of starchy food. I always enjoyed the bread and butter puddings and the rice puddings and went back for seconds. The food wasn't too bad. No wonder I was called *tjuni pulka*[3] and *pungyn*[4].

There were days when we were treated to home-made pasties, made especially for us by one of the older Colebrook cooks whom we called Grandpa. I don't remember this man's name but I do remember him being dressed in white in the kitchen, making enough pasties for everyone. If any were left over, we were allowed to take them to school the next day. We thought that was great.

We could hear the baker coming through the huge gates. The sound of the horses' hooves on the gravel made us all come alive with excitement as we ran with the horses trying to get into the cart to pinch the crumbs off the floor. Just the smell of the fresh bread made us feel hungry. When the baker had gathered the loaves and placed them in his huge cane baskets, we all scampered onto the cart and tried to devour as many fresh crumbs as possible. We quickly dug holes into the freshly baked bread and then ran for our lives as soon as we heard someone coming, making sure that we wouldn't get caught.

---

3 tjuni pulka: fat
4 pungyn: greedy

The pig man, as we called him, was a regular visitor. He collected the leftover food scraps in huge drums. The drums were then taken to a nearby farm. We always stood around watching him as he heaved these enormous drums with ease.

There are many good memories of our home. The verandahs of the big house were supported by rows of great posts and we had the pleasure of weaving and running in and out of this grand home and into the gardens. We hid and played in and about the hedges out in the front of this wonderful building. We didn't play much in the front garden but I often sat on the girls' side of the verandah either dreaming or talking to myself or playing the mouth organ.

I was a sooky but I was also a tomboy. I kicked the football, climbed trees, played marbles and had games of knucklebones. I was constantly teased by the older girls. If I had cut myself, the girls immediately chanted, 'Doris Kartinyeri, you're going to die. Doris Kartinyeri you're going to die.' I ran crying to the staff. One of the older girls always got me by the britches and dragged me until I yelled out for help. This was rather painful and embarrassing.

During primary school we walked to school and home again. Us *maru* kids used to always find something to amuse ourselves both at school and at home. We had the greatest pleasure in inventing our own games. Some of the things we used to get into would make you shiver. One of the boys decided that he was superman, so he climbed the bloody roof. He jumped and broke a leg.

We often played our favourite game, 'Kick the Tin'. We really enjoyed the game, which I have already described. It was a game Sister Hyde brought back from Melbourne and introduced to us. We never got bored with this particular game. Brandy was also another game we played a lot. We played football and cricket and then of course hopscotch. We'd mark the hopscotch games with a stick in the dirt. We'd kick our legs high in the air. Our legs grey with dust. We shared our laughter in these games, sitting in the dirt. When we didn't have the good old knucklebones to play with, we used stones. We enjoyed playing in the dirt and using our imagination to make up games.

We collected the lids off the jam tins and made tin whistles. We'd force the lid in half, being careful not to cut ourselves on the sharp and jagged edges and then pierce a hole through it with a rusty old nail and rock. Then put our fingers in the opening, blowing hard to develop a whistle. Maybe my follow-up book could be called *The Tin Whistle* or *Knuckle Bones*. The good old humble jam tin certainly came in handy. Not only did we have tin whistles and 'Kick the Tin', we also made telephones and tin stilts out of them. We had a lot of fun chasing or running around the place with these tins under our feet. They made us feel tall and proud, giggling and laughing as we chased each other around the yard. We made a game with almost anything.

We had enormous amounts of land to venture into the scrub and to play our games. I remember a particular area that was a wetland. There we looked for frogs and tadpoles. We played in the water and tried to float an old windmill where we'd sit balancing ourselves and getting soaking wet.

There were times when we gathered up old sheets of galvanised iron to slide down the hills towards the railway lines. We found an old wood shed. It was a good place to romp around and play our imaginative games and, at the same time, look for *maku*[5]. We gathered wood to build a truck. The driver and passengers in the back pretended to drive along.

We tinkered with inventive toys. We made a thing out of buttons by pulling a piece of cotton through the button holes and then pulled on each end forming a motion like a yo-yo, moving both hands in and out as

---

5 maku: witchetty grub

the button spun around. There was another game I can recall made out of a button, rubber band and a hair-clip. By threading the rubber band through the buttonholes, tying both ends to the hair-clip and then twisting the button on the rubber band as tight as we could, it formed a spring reaction. This was then placed in a closed book, which was presented to some unsuspecting person, and then we'd wait for their shocked reaction. We watched them open the book up carefully, then jump back in amazement and fright. We often played this trick on the kids at school. Black buttons were most effective as they looked more like a spider springing out of the books. This was one of our favourite games. It scared the living daylights out of them.

Music meant a lot to us. We had plenty of it and enjoyed singing, even if it was hymns. I enjoyed the mouth organ and I played it sitting cross-legged on the verandah on the girls' side of the dormitories. Again, most of the tunes were hymns. I reckon if I was given a mouth organ one day, I could give out one hell of a bash, playing the old hymns. A couple of the older girls taught themselves to play the piano by ear. Auntie Dora, one of the older girls, played the piano so well that she eventually attended the Conservatory of Music at Adelaide University.

Our feet were never still. Even while waiting for our turn at hopscotch or other games, we danced around in the dirt. Magpies flying in rhythm to our dancing feet.

DANCING IN THE WIND

Laughter is on the wind.
Dance little ones, dance.
Reach for the skies.

The wind is mighty
Dance little ones
Let me hear your
Colebrook feet.

I can remember how some of the older boys would put their heads on the railway tracks and listen for the trains. Sometimes they played chicken with the oncoming trains. They placed rocks on the railway line and raced away when they heard a train coming. Maybe they thought they could derail the train. Once the train had passed, the boys ran as fast as they could and jumped on the end of the carriage for a joyride to the next station.

The older boys used to look for rabbit holes and then put their hands in the burrows and fetch out the young kittens. We held them for a while and then put them back. We weren't afraid of anything that crawled. We entertained ourselves with lots of interesting things, even putting or poking sticks down the trapdoor spiders' holes. We weren't afraid of being adventurous and daring. Every day was an adventure, full of excitement and new challenges without any major injuries.

There were days when we were treated to horse rides. We ran to meet the owners of the horses. Kicking our heels in the dirt, we waited for our turn to mount the horses and did so with great difficulty. Grinning excitedly, we enjoyed being led around the tennis court.

On the weekends, we went for walks. Sometimes we went to Sturt Creek for a swim. Arriving at our destination, we refreshed ourselves from the long walk and the heat by swimming fully clothed in the waterfall. I always dreaded the thought of having to dry off on the huge rocks, knowing that it was time to venture back up the treacherous hills that were cruel to us. Trudging the steep hills, we soon felt the heat again as we slowly left the creek behind with our wet clothes clinging to us.

Going to our secret gardens with the other girls was special. On warm spring afternoons we were allowed to go for a walk in the hills and gather wild flowers. We gathered small daisies to make daisy chains. We'd sit in the tall grasses, gleefully putting the stems together, making our necklaces or wristbands. At the secret gardens, which were our pride, we each dug a hole and placed a pretty picture or flower in the hole and carefully covered our treasures with a piece of clear jagged glass. The ritual was finalised by burying everything under a layer of soil. If flowers were not available, we placed a picture in the spot after carefully removing the dirt off the glass. Then there were other times when we gathered small bunches of tall green grass seed and wrapped the buds with pretty silver paper, admiring our work of art. We regularly checked on our buried treasures. Our thin cotton dresses never stayed clean for long and were always covered in fine dust whenever we played in our secret gardens. Even though our dresses were thin and cotton we always wore aprons. I don't know whether this was to keep us warm or clean!

We gathered all sorts of bush tucker, many berries and *maku*. We picked chow, which is a sticky gum from certain trees. We put the gum in a jar of hot water to soften it and chew to our hearts content, ending up with our mouths full of sticky gum and juice dribbling down our faces. There were also times when we looked for yallacus in the nearby paddocks. Yallacus were small brown-coloured bulbs with white centres. They were soft shelled and easy to peel. The white centres were quite tasteless but nevertheless we enjoyed eating them. We'd dig for them in sandy spots, ending up getting covered in fine grey dust. There was a small plant with a long stem with a small green pod which was tasteless. We called it 'maize'. We used to pick these both at the home and in the school ground. Monkey nuts were also plentiful. These fell from the pine trees. We were never short of bush tucker. Looking back now, I am amazed at our natural instinct for bush food. We had our heritage taken from us but we still had the natural instinct for finding the right foods. None of the children suffered illness from the food we discovered.

I remember some visitors coming to the home and a white man telling Dennis, one of the boys, that if he ate a raw witchety grub he would give him two shillings. Dennis had a big dimple in his cheek and he smiled with a huge grin showing his pearly white teeth against his beautiful dark skin. We all stood around laughing and giggling with approval and encouragement. Dennis ate the *maku* gleefully and said, 'proper *palya*[6].'

Our days were never dull as we always had plenty to do. We picked blackberries at Sturt Creek. The walk there seemed long and we swam in the creek. As soon as we arrived we tossed a sheet of galvanised iron over the blackberry bush and picked buckets of blackberries, usually eating more than we took home. We all wandered back home through the shrubs and bushes and climbed above the cliffs, looking back wearily with our scratches and purple hands and carrying our few berries in bags or tins.

Back row (L–R): Avis Edwards, Margaret Apma, Sister Lovibond, Christine Pinkie, Joan Giles.
Front row (L–R): Doris Kartinyeri, Ray Argent (deceased) nursing David James, Dennis Rankine (deceased), Francis Mchughes (deceased), and Billy Forbes.

6 palya: good

Drawing by Chris

The Colebrook Tree
Designed by Faith Thomas

THE ROOTS represent the many tribes the children originated from.

THE TRUNK represents the love and devotion of Sister Hyde and Sister Rutter. Their caring formed us into a strong family unit.

THE BRANCHES indicate the family branching out into their individual lives.

THE LEAVES represent the many Colebrook offspring but mainly the Colebrook umbrella portrays the strong moral values instilled in us by Sisters Hyde and Rutter which have shielded us through life.

THE BEGINNING OF GRIEF

'After (the Sisters) left those kids went through hell on earth. They had to rely on each other to survive.'
Auntie Faith Thomas

In 1952, after many years of devotion and caring for the children, Sister Hyde and Sister Rutter both left Colebrook to establish a hostel for the senior girls. Their departure left me shattered. When the time came for them to leave, everyone was very sad. I can still see myself partly hidden in the bushes standing alone and crying softly, feeling left out on their departure. It was a sad occasion as they left with the older girls for Parkside to open a hostel called Tanderra. I felt I would never see them again.

After Sister Hyde and Sister Rutter left, we had a continuous change of staff. Things began to change drastically. Religion was practised more frequently. We were submitted to a stricter routine but we still had the privileges of going for long walks, looking for wild flowers or blackberries, swimming at Sturt Creek. We could still go gathering mushrooms and bush tucker.

Even though our life was regimented and strict, it taught us to share and be one big extended family.

Because religion was so important to the new superintendent, his wife and their family, we were made to practise at the home and whenever we went out. It was all in the hands of the Lord. Praise the Lord! Hallelujah! It was God's will to practise religion, wherever we went, whether it was to the beach or the zoo or any other public place. We found this most embarrassing and humiliating. Grace was said before and after meals, as we had to thank the Lord for everything. We all sang in harmony, sometimes mockingly, looking around carefully and making sure that we were not caught. The religious strictness was phenomenal. It was supposed to be for our own good. I believe these people thought they were called by the Lord to become missionaries and to care for us, the Aboriginal children. The stolen Aboriginal children.

There was a lady who mainly looked after the girls. We could hear her coming towards the dormitories with her heels pit-a-patting on the verandah, going from room to room, checking on us. One of her duties was to settle us for the night. I can remember her at nights as she was kneeling and praying at the end of our beds, nodding off to sleep as she plucked her eyebrows with her fingers. She hardly had any eyebrows. It used to frighten me as she dozed off, nodding her head sitting in the dark, this shadow. I thought there was something terribly wrong with her. I thought she was ill. Another of her duties was to wake the girls in the early hours of the morning to use the 'chambers', potties, for us to avoid wetting the beds. I dreaded the cold wintry mornings, as the potties were cold and cruel on our *mana*[7]. This was one of her ritual duties that was done every night and morning. I did have a soft spot for her and her 'God Bless Girls', as she left the rooms.

I hated Sundays for we could not do a thing. It was sinful to involve yourself in any activities on the Lord's Day. The Bible was read a lot. We had no television or wireless. We were punished if we stepped out of line. It was a day just for worship and no play. Church services were held three times a day. We were brainwashed. Is this called religion? We were just young children for God's sake.

Each Sunday began with breakfast and blessings. We dressed up in our Sunday best clothes and prepared ourselves for a long walk to the church. The sister strutted quickly in front of us, dressed in low-heel shoes, a staid dress, felt hat and carrying a small

---

7 mana: buttocks, bottom

vinyl bag. When we were allowed to wear seamed stockings, one of the girls was reprimanded for skipping along in her high heels and stockings. She was told to act like a lady and not gallop around like a horse. We all thought we looked pretty flash in our Sunday clothes. To us it was an outing and a time to have a sip of the Holy Communion wine and have a taste of the Holy Bread, which tasted better each time. Then the collection plate was passed from row to row. When we sang 'Hear the pennies dropping, listen while they fall' this was the time to pinch a few coins and we quickly moved into action. It gave us time away from the home but we returned to more religion being thrust upon us.

In the evenings, we had a film night or concerts that the various churches put on for us, or the usual Bible Studies. The home was blessed with donations. Various churches visited on Harvest Thanksgiving Day in the name of the Lord. The donations delivered on a Sunday evening were in such abundance, our mouths watered for the water melons and food stuff. There was always plenty of fruit and vegetables.

Grote Street Church of Christ was a place where some of the children were baptised. At my baptism, my sister Margaret was being baptised too. I was dressed in this white cotton gown and I felt strange.

Dressed in our Sunday best
Back row (L–R): Elsa Cooper, Wendy Waye, Patricia Waye,
Christine Pinkie.
Front row (L–R): Doris Kartinyeri, Margaret Apma, Joan Giles,
Avis Edwards.

I almost had a mishap and nearly slipped over as I was walking down toward the baptismal font. It was my turn to be cleansed of my sins, so I was told by the staff of the home. Did I really and fully understand what was happening to me? No!

After each evening meal we were given a Bible quiz. If you returned the right answer you were rewarded with a lolly. We all raced into our dormitories diving for our personal Bible, all searching for the right answers. After all the pushing and shoving, we would end up back in the dining room, reaching out to the Superintendent who must have thought he was someone special like Jesus Christ. He would reach over us, rewarding each kid with a lolly for the right answer. This occurred a few times a week or when the Superintendent felt generous. That power over us was unyielding. We were powerless.

I have memories of busloads of people passing by the home. They were known to us as 'Good Samaritans'. They didn't stop in their travels on their way to or from their picnics. From the bus windows, they threw lollies out at us. Young as we were, we scrambled to pick them up. Lollies were such a treat. Didn't these people feel any shame treating us like animals?

The lolly man was different. Every Saturday afternoon all us *maru* kids waited in anticipation for the lolly man. We sat on the verandah and looked anxiously down the road for Mr. Mitchell who would be carrying his brown kit bag. Once he had arrived, we all gathered around him nervously, pulling at him, eagerly wanting what he brought for us. He had every possible lolly you could think of from Fantales to Minties and good old Walking Sticks. Mr. Mitchell knew us all by name and knew exactly what our needs were. He did this as a genuine act of kindness, not as a reward for quoting verses from the Bible, parrot fashion. He made sure that none of the children missed out. We will always remember Mr. Mitchell.

Hygiene was taught to all the children. We had to have our daily showers. If you had nits you were forced to have your hair shaved and to wear a small cap, both at home and at school. The kids were teased, which was humiliating for all concerned.

There were children who suffered with ear problems and they had to line up to have their ears literally flushed out with warm water and oil once or twice a week. Some of the children had their ears tortured daily with horrible, huge, cold syringes. These children suffered severe ear infections and needed medical treatment. They were forced to put up with these barbaric treatments. Many of the children never recovered from this terrible ordeal and suffered permanent deafness or continuing ear problems. The staff member responsible wasn't even trained. My God! Who gave them the right to practice this sort of barbaric treatment on innocent children? As the kids lined up, we watched as each child went through their ordeal. It was distressing to see them cringe with pain. I was fortunate not to have problems with my ears.

We were dressed in our second-hand clothes, always wearing aprons, sometimes looking like raggedy Annies, but we knew no different. The shoes we wore were usually hand-me-downs and weren't particularly comfortable. They were either too tight or too big. Sometimes we received new pairs of lace-ups and then showed off by deliberately making them squeak as we walked around the home and our classrooms, making sure that they squeaked loud enough for us to be noticed. We giggled to ourselves as we walked past any-body. I have suffered tremendously with bad feet all my life and my doctor says this is a result of wearing poor shoes. Consequently I have had to go into hospital to have an operation on both my feet.

We all had duties to perform every weekend. The roster was always made up for us to comply with, so the chores could be done in an orderly manner.

On a Saturday morning the bedrooms and the commonroom floors had to be washed and polished. The rooms were stripped of their furniture, which was put out in the courtyard. The chores were done with great enthusiasm. The commonroom used to be polished by hand covering every inch with a dark coloured polish. The floors were washed and polished by us on our knees. We got covered with water and

(L–R): Doris Kartinyeri, Irene Marks (deceased), Margaret Long.

floor polish. The best part was when we skated around the rooms in our socks, buffing the floor with our *tjina*[8], bursting with laughter. I think we had more polish on us than the damn floors.

There was always plenty of laughter when doing our chores and then being sidetracked into doing other mischievous things, like teasing an older girl who had a dog. We teased the dog until it started barking,

---

8 tjina: feet

then we ran for the nearest cupboard to hide and continued teasing the dog.

At the home we had an older Aboriginal lady, Adeline, who had two small children, David and Alice. She had the duty of doing chores in the laundry and sorting the piles of clean clothes. In the linen room there were two huge presses for the sheets that were fed through manually and with great difficulty, using one hand to turn the handle. The clothes were sorted, folded and placed in order for each child. We had no wardrobes but the walls were lined with shelves for our clothes. The women from the churches came to the home to do the mending of the clothes and darn socks.

One day I was just messing around with the old wringer washing machine when I got my arm caught. The machine was similar to the presser but this was an electric one and my arm moved faster. I managed to pull it out with great effort and pain. I stuffed up the rollers in the machine as well as having a sore arm for a while. I didn't tell anyone though. Shamed and scared!

The old copper was lit and the linen boiled while Adeline poked the linen with a huge wooden copper stick. We watched Adeline struggling as she hung the linen. The dazzling white sheets billowing in the breeze could be seen from miles away. The laundry was filled with the smell of the hot refreshing steam. The copper flickered all day till dusk. This was when we took advantage of the hot coals.

We put our stolen goodies, potatoes and sugar in to cook in the burning fire. The sweet fragrance of the sugar lingered in the laundry as it slowly turned into toffee in the old lids of boot polish tins that sat awkwardly on the glowing coals. Even though the toffees were often slightly burnt we enjoyed them. The stolen potatoes also ended up in the ashes under the old copper. We burned our fingers trying to devour the hot potatoes as quickly as possible before we got caught. Luckily we never were. With the copper door open we sat watching the flames flicker in the stillness of the night, keeping ourselves warm, moving around quietly and giggling to ourselves with our little goodies.

Washing the dishes was the girls' chore. We were all subjected to chores in the scullery, taking turns in collecting all the dishes that were passed through the servery window and making sure that everything was left clean. I didn't mind doing the dishes, as it was a good opportunity to steal from the pantry. However, I did get caught once with a mouthful of Sunshine powdered milk as I was doing the chores in the kitchen. I couldn't swallow it and it just swelled up in my mouth. I almost choked to death on all this dried powdered milk. I had no choice but to blow it out. It sprayed from my mouth, going everywhere. Some of it remained sticking to the roof of my mouth, which made it really difficult for me to explain. I got a hell of a hiding. We stole other things as well—condensed milk, sugar and potatoes. One of the girls had a thing about condensed milk. She was always seen sipping from the tin by the other girls. She hid in the toilets and continued sipping from her tin. We used to have small bottles of coke delivered. They also went missing. Even though we only received the small bottles, it was a real treat. It was just enough to get a taste of the gassy fizz. We never got caught or punished.

A few of the older girls joined up with the local Girls Life Brigade. My memories are a little vague but a group of girls and I would get ready, in our uniforms, feeling pretty flash with our polished shoes and neat tie. We were met by the white members of the brigade and went to the Blackwood Church of Christ on Friday nights. On weekends we went camping. One night, we were followed up to the hall by an Aboriginal man, a full-blood, who said he was the father of one of the girls with us. We were scared and ran. She didn't accept that he was her father.

Religion became the main issue within Colebrook. I remember that Saturday nights were outings for some of the children. Whoever was chosen was told to get ready and they dressed for a train trip to Adelaide to attend the Rechabite Hall for a Christian convention. It was a ritual event to attend these services. We not only went to the Rechabite Hall. We also visited the Billy Graham Crusades. I enjoyed going to the conventions. It was a good time to take advantage of the train rides. It was a long night and we got home late.

On boarding the train, then hearing the sound of the click-clack and feeling the movement of the train, the adrenalin raced as we neared the tunnel. The smell of the smoke coming from the train was strong. After the tunnel, we were confronted with this huge screen, a drive-in theatre, we were not permitted to look at. It was evil, so they told us. We were made to sit on the right-hand-side of the aisle. It's not so amazing that, with our regular train rides from Eden Hills to Adelaide, we could name all the stations off by heart.

Arriving at the Adelaide Station, we would meet some of the Aboriginals who gathered in a group around the Station. On seeing us, they immediately moved slowly towards us then introduced themselves as our cousin or uncle or 'lation (relation). We hung our heads feeling shame. The rail station and the River Torrens were the meeting places for Aboriginal people.

Many of the children who went on train trips enjoyed the atmosphere of the Conventions, which were so tremendous that the impressions last until today. At Colebrook we learnt many hymns. These hymns and the sound of joyful voices still ring in my ears. We still recite some of the hymns and choruses that were taught to us. Because of the continuous Bible-bashing and brainwashing, we are able to recite today the books of the Bible and know many hymns by heart like 'Jesus loves the little children, all the children of the world'. Many songs are still with us. We often sang in harmony. Today I can still sing the books of the Bible.

ALL TOGETHER NOW!

Genesis, Exodus, Leviticus
Numbers, Deuteronomy,
Joshua, Judges, Ruth
First And Second Samuel
Kings, Kings, Chronicles and Chronicles,
Ezra, Nehemiah, Esther, Job,

Forget the bloody rest!

There were some children who were favoured and others who, for some unknown reason, were treated badly. But we supported one another. We always knew who wet the bed from the boys' dormitory. They were outside in the cold, peeling potatoes in the early hours of the morning, preparing vegetables for the evening meal. The other bed-wetters could be punished by standing for all meals and eating dry weetbix. Then they were punished by having cold showers. To me this was physical and mental abuse. These punishments must have had an effect on the individuals later in life. The staff had a great influence on us and I believe that they have a lot to answer for. The strictness affected many of our brothers and sisters. This is one of the reasons I believe a majority of our sisters and brothers went to either gaol or mental institutions. Others suffered with alcoholism. All in the name of Religion!

For a short time there was a school at Colebrook because the parents of the children at Eden Hills Primary School refused to have us *maru* kids there. During the days of Sister Hyde and Sister Rutter, I remember our classroom was set up in the main dining room. Our teacher was a local lady who lived across the road. Later on, the school was not viable at the home and we were all finally able to go to the Eden Hills Primary School. We had no transport but walking long distances every day didn't seem to bother us.

My schooling at Eden Hills was enjoyable. The children from the home had their own friends, and I was able to mix in well with the white children too. Lunch times we sat on the ground eating our sandwiches and picking maize at the same time. I recall how we squeezed our sandwiches, letting the jam ooze down our fingers, licking the sticky warm jam as it melted in our hands. Our vegemite sandwiches also ended up like this. Making the sandwiches in the early hours of the morning was one of the chores the girls had to do.

My best friend at school was a girl named Adrienne. We nicknamed her Smashy. She always sat with me. I tried to swap my sandwiches with her and have her recess cake as well, if I could. We never had the small luxuries of cakes for recess. We often asked the white kids for their morning recess cake. We only had the same boring bloody sandwiches, either vegemite or hot apricot jam, or the warm fritz and sauce sandwiches. So you can imagine what they were like by recess time, and understand why we all tried to swap them with the white children. There were several white kids in the neighbourhood who played with us after school.

Some of the children received pocket money, depending on their behaviour or age. If you were fortunate you'd receive two shillings, threepence, sixpence or one shilling to spend at the local tucker shop near the school. If the money wasn't spent, then we had it taken off us. The little tuck shop had all the assorted lollies that you can't find today. I do remember when we all had a personal bank account and we proudly deposited threepence a week or a penny. To us that was a lot of money. I quite often wonder whatever happened to our bank accounts!

I wasn't good at school but I did enjoy reading. My first primer I cherished, especially the quotation, 'Words are just like stepping stones to lead you on your way'. I disliked arithmetic and always found myself cheating in class when it came time for my brain to add or subtract. I enjoyed being with my close friends at school but I didn't feel as if I was bright. I barely made it through primary and I dreaded the idea of going to high school, especially the thought of mixing with kids that I didn't know.

A lot of white people who came to visit us at Colebrook did not know why we were there—that we had been stolen from our families and placed there.

On Sunday afternoons some of the children had their relatives come and visit. I remember three old ladies who we called Auntie. We sat on the front verandah waiting in anticipation. I have lasting impressions of our Aunts. They always found time for all the children. Although we all loved to see Aunt Undahlia, Aunt Lammo, and Aunt Chickenna striding proudly towards the home, climbing the hilly winding road, at the same time we were too shy to express our feelings.

On some occasions, we were visited by our parents. My father visited me at Colebrook. I waited on the verandah steps while he slowly plodded up the hill towards me. My father was a stout man. He was a handsome man. He wore a brown felt hat with a broad brim. His silvery grey hair shone. I especially liked his smile. It made me feel special. As I sat with him on the front verandah, it was difficult for me to call my father 'Dad'. If I wanted to connect with him, it was always a nudge or a 'hey'. My Dad sat me on his lap and then I asked him shyly, 'gimme two bob please'. He would slip two shillings into my hands. This was a lot of money so I saved it for the tucker shop near my school. I remember going to the zoo in Adelaide on one occasion with my father and a cousin of mine.

During my father's visits to Colebrook, there was no mention of my mother or of her death, nor did I ask. I had lost my culture and language. The word 'mother' did not have any meaning for me. I just did not know the word. I vividly remember using my pillow to cuddle at night for comfort and security. Even though my brothers and sisters accompanied my father on his visits, I felt no bond with them. Doreen said, 'I am your sister' and I replied, 'No, you're not my sister! These are my brothers and sisters here.' Doreen was very upset that my ties were with the Colebrook brothers and sisters. Much later I had the feeling that my father was an angry man. I can understand why he was angry. Eventually, as I matured and got to know my natural family, we became very close and a strong bond developed.

Cracker Night! The appearance of three-penny bombs, jumping jacks, catherine wheels and sparklers heralded the up-coming Guy Fawkes night. Cracker Night, as we called it, saw all of us kids collecting wood and any other combustibles and building a gigantic bonfire. The day couldn't go fast enough for darkness to come and the lighting of the fire. We all waited in anticipation for our guests to arrive. As they arrived in droves, the families met us and the Superintendent selected the children to be placed into family groups. As huge bonfires were being built, the dark skies lit up as we ran around holding on tightly to the sparklers. The banging of the fireworks scared us as we lingered playing in the dark. The colourful displays and explosion of the crackers offered a brief respite from the regimentation of religious instructions and devotions. Roll on next year!

The bus trips to the beach were something we all looked forward to. We always seemed to go to the same beach, at Brighton or Grange. Our beach days began with preparing cut lunches, then the arrival of the bus. We all clambered onto the bus with great enthusiasm, fighting over which seat we had, all wanting the seats nearest the windows.

When we prepared to go for our swim, we undressed in a most discreet manner, not showing our bodies off too much as we were told it was sinful to do so. We felt real shame. We had to change as quickly as possible. As soon as we came out of the water, we were marched up to the change rooms with towels draped around us. Before lunch we had to say grace aloud and in unison. 'For what we are about to receive, Lord make us truly thankful. Amen.' Then there was the

Bible reading and singing grace in unison again after dinner was eaten to thank the Lord for what we had received. To all of us, this was the most embarrassing and humiliating thing we had to do. We all hung our heads in shame. This was the practice at all our outings—to the zoo, the National Parks or wherever we went. The graces are still singing in my ears even today. 'Hallelujah Amen'.

The visits to the Adelaide Zoo was always memorable. We had time to take a look at old George the gorilla and feed him, poking fun at him, as he tossed his Hexham bag towards us begging for food. We always had packed lunches but I cannot remember ever having fruit like bananas or oranges. One of the boys named George Rankine, nicknamed 'Bulldog', would call out 'Come and get your 'happles', everybody! Come and get your 'happles'.' We girls teased George chanting aloud, 'Georgie Porgy kissed the girls and made them cry.' George, our brother has passed on now. He will always be in our hearts.

There were regular trips to the National Parks. We were packed on trucks like sardines going on a picnic. There were times we went to various churches as invited guests to sing hymns.

The many visits to the Adelaide Dental Clinic were excuses to stay away from school. Our visits began with the kids being told. Then they would leave on this old Ford buckboard, on their merry way to the dentist in the big city. My visit to the Children's Hospital was a laugh. I pretended to be sick, supposed to be suffering with appendicitis. I put on a real good turn! My hospital stay wasn't pleasant though. I received the normal treatments, then was allowed to leave the next day. Just to stay away from school! It worked. They found nothing wrong.

At least one night a week we had film evenings. When I was much younger, before the change of staff, we were visited by the Apex Club. They showed good movies such as *The Three Stooges* and *The Rascals*. But with the tougher discipline of the new staff, we were only allowed to watch slides of ourselves on the screen, followed by a scroll film based on stories from the Bible. We were always provided with food from various churches and social groups. God willing!

During the week our evenings involved Bible studies, or some of the local churches visiting for various functions. On one occasion I recall being in a prayer meeting and peeping through my hands listening to one of the Sisters from the kitchen talking about the food. A social group had delivered trays of food and it was rejected because it was brought from a party. This was not acceptable. It was not 'Gods Will' so it was evil to accept foods from such functions. This must have been so humiliating for that group. I watched with dismay and disbelief as the food was repacked and carried out of the kitchen. I was thinking only of my stomach when I should have been in prayer. That's all I was thinking of, food, food, food, *tjuni pulka*. 'Praise the Lord'. Amen!

Once I went for my holidays at Christmas to a young married European couple. They welcomed me with open arms. They both made me feel wanted by giving me plenty of hugs. They couldn't do enough for me. I was ten years old at that time. Their culture was completely different to mine. The Christmas tree was decorated with fruit or biscuits, which weren't the usual decorations for me to see. I enjoyed the holiday, but I was always glad to get back to the home.

Another time I went for a holiday with a blind couple, Mr and Mrs Pierce. This was a real experience for me, as I had to get used to the idea of sitting in the dark. The blind couple hadn't realised that I needed light. It was marvellous watching Mr and Mrs Pierce coping with their daily chores, totally blind. They were a religious couple who read the Bible in Braille. My stay was brief but it was a change.

The yearly trip to Mount Breckan for the Christmas party was a special event to look forward to. The long trip was a good time for us all to sing hymns as we travelled on the bus. Then there were times that we sang our made up versions of songs, giggling amongst ourselves as we sang. On arrival, we were welcomed by the Apex club who organised, what seemed to us then, a big and wonderful Christmas party. The whole place seemed huge to us with plenty of ground space surrounding a castle-like building. I always looked forward to seeing Father Christmas appearing up through the chimney, waving down to us as we waved back to him. We greeted him in anticipation of our Christmas stocking.

We always received good quality toys. The girls received a quite sturdy toy, like a clothes hoist. We were told to check our Christmas stockings, then throw any toy lipsticks or any other so called 'evil things' out of the window on the way home. So out the window went these harmless toys. It didn't bother us. The lipstick was small and make believe and, after all, it didn't make me beautiful.

Christmas to most people means St Nicholas coming down the chimney, stockings and marsh-mallows. But to us, the phrase 'Merry Xmas' brought the wrath of God upon us. The word 'Christ' was left out of Christmas. This aspect of Christmas had a nullifying affect on us *maru* kids of what Christmas was all about. We did celebrate Christmas each year. I recall being given plain white pillowcases, to be filled by the Superintendent with Christmas toys. Then we had our yearly visits to the Christmas Pageant and the multicultural Christmas dinner at the Adelaide Town Hall. All the institutions around Adelaide were guests on this occasion.

I have learned from a friend that children from the local Sunday School who brought us gifts at Christmas were told that these poor children were orphans and had no families. Another white lie. Why couldn't they have told the Sunday School children the real stories behind these children's faces?

Because religion was so important to the staff, the children were not taught about basic things, like sexuality. I had crushes on some of the boys, both at school and at the home. We used to hold hands under the desk. We were innocent and curious but we didn't know any different. It was just a part of growing up, with a strict Christian upbringing. Sex was all a taboo. We were never taught about life.

My first memory with sexual awareness was in the home. Both Sisters Hyde and Rutter had already left. I vividly remember an old white man who was employed at the home. He had the habit of urinating around the home. We often caught him in the front garden. I and a group of other girls watched him from the dining room windows as we giggled amongst ourselves.

As an individual child with no family there to protect me, and being black, naive and vulnerable, I was easy prey for the sexual predators. Colebrook seemed to be a haven for sexual deviants. It was a terrible place to live for a lot of the children.

We had many changes of staff within the home and some of them were not the best. As children, we were robbed of our personal rights. The promiscuity of the staff was inflicted on some of the children. I was enticed into some ungodly behaviour with a senior staff member. In the evenings we had prayer meetings or a film night. You couldn't afford to be sick. The night of the film evenings we all ran for chairs and I was always enticed to sit next to this so called religious woman, only to be subjected to her personal desires. She reached for my hand to place between her legs to fondle the upper parts. This continued for a long while, whenever we had film evenings. Can you imagine how I felt—being alone, with no one to talk to about these horrific things happening to me?

When the time came for us to leave Colebrook some were fortunate to go back to their people. Many had to deal with lots of prejudice and opposition but eventually went on to achieve good employment positions in the community. Some became nurses, teachers, social workers, ministers, actors, artists, writers, sportspersons, tradespeople and administrators. Today these people are held with great respect and praised in our community. Dr Lowitja O'Donoghue is a great source of inspiration to the many former Colebrook residents. As Auntie Lowitja said herself, 'We were only prepared for domestic work but they couldn't keep us down.' Her work as Chairperson of ATSIC as well as in many other community organisations has made her famous. Lowitja was Australian of the Year in 1988 and some of us went to Melbourne to see her get the CBE award. Yami Lester has also done extremely important work as Director of the Pitjanjatjarra Council. One of my Colebrook brothers, Jacob Stengle, has become well known nationally and internationally for his artwork.

Years have passed and we have lost quite a few brothers. It is good to have the Colebrook reunions and reminisce about the old days at Colebrook.

Back row (L–R): Christine Pinkie, Elsa Cooper, May James.
Middle row (L–R): Doris Kartinyeri, Norveen Turner, Margaret Apma.
Front row (L–R): Dary Wilson (deceased).

SHUNTED ABOUT

It was decided I was to leave Colebrook when I was fourteen. I didn't know why. It was a sad occasion for me to leave all my brothers and sisters behind. This was a place dear to my heart. I was removed once again by the Protection Board and placed in a white family home. It was a whole new environment for me, living in a family of four white children and one adopted Aboriginal child.

I continued to go to school and attended the Unley Girls Technical High School. I had a few friends at the school. My feelings about school were negative and not productive. Again, where is the guiding hand a child is meant to have? My attendance was good but my grades weren't successful. I just did not like the academic part of school. I was teased at school. I hated dressmaking but I did like cooking classes. As I look back I realise that it wasn't completely fulfilling.

I had to travel on my bike a long distance from Edwardstown to Unley, many times running late.

Riding to school each day gave me a sense of responsibility and independence as well as a time to daydream. I knew all the back roads, avoiding traffic or dogs that always knew when I was coming. I had one hell of an accident on my damn bike. Coming down the road was a busload of *marus*. I had never seen so many and this fascinated me so much that I ended up in the back of a trailer full of debris, badly gashing my leg. I was in agony. It was not long before someone came to my aid and I was soon at the doctor's getting stitched up.

I was able to visit an Aboriginal family whom I met on my travels. The family lived in a wooden frame railway house. Elsie and her husband Fred were hard workers. He worked for the railways for a long time. On a wet day it was an excuse to stop at the house for shelter. If I missed school I went there. I was always welcomed into the house and as it turned out, Elsie, the mother of the children, was my cousin. When I said shyly that my name was Doris Kartinyeri, she knew all my family. This was my first contact with my people after leaving the home and my cousin became excited as she welcomed me with a big grin.

The house was always warm and Elsie always had simple hot meals cooked on the wood stove. The smell of the hot damper lingered in the small house. The old copper in the laundry smelt of fresh soapy steam. I often visited them after school. I enjoyed becoming part of the happy atmosphere and their free and easy lifestyle. In particular I enjoyed the scones and stews that my cousin cooked on the wood stove. I would leave the house feeling quite pleased in myself. Riding home on my bike I made no mention of these regular stops to the white family.

On many occasions I was horrified by a man who repeatedly exposed himself to me. This totally shocked me. It was so humiliating. I would be running late for school, waiting for this man to pump up my bike tyres. Here was this man in his pyjamas fully exposing himself while fixing my damn bike. I looked away, knowing and thinking that he was deliberately doing this to me. I rode off to school feeling perplexed and angry. This caused me to have a sense of insecurity after I left for school.

I think the best thing that happened to me while I was still at school was when I found a hundred pounds rolled up in notes in a bundle. I took the money to the Unley Police Station. It was never claimed and I had to pay ten shillings to reclaim it. I don't remember spending the money.

I was not doing well at school. Struggling with the travelling by bike and the extra studies became too much. I didn't receive any encouragement for my schoolwork from the white family I lived with. Homework wasn't a regular practice. Religion was more important than education. The man and his wife decided it would be better for me to leave school and do housework.

Once I left high school I began the task of housekeeping for this family I lived with. My duties were to look after the four kids, prepare meals and general housekeeping. I was about fourteen at this time. I knew little about cooking. When I was asked to put potatoes on, I did just that—put a saucepan full of potatoes on the stove to boil with no bloody water. I worked here for cheap labour as a domestic. No money was ever exchanged.

I attended the local church for youth group and Bible studies or a game of tennis. Youth group was in the evenings in the middle of the week at the church hall. Afterwards my friends and I took walks to local shops for fish and chips. I made some good friends at the youth group. I even remember them giving me a birthday party. The youth group bought me a yellow cardigan. I attended the local church and Sunday school and played tennis on the weekends for the church group. I enjoyed playing tennis and was good at it. But most importantly, I attended church every Sunday.

Next I was taken blindly without any explanation from the Edwardstown family to a house in the hills at Coromandel Valley not far from Colebrook. This was a traumatic removal for me once again. I felt isolated. I lived in horrible cold quarters separated from the house about thirty yards. They were poorly lit and at night it was pitch dark. I used to be scared coming back after doing the dinner dishes.

Here was this lay minister of the church who I soon experienced as a man who constantly exposed himself to me. At night I could hear him at my bedroom window. I lay in bed frigid with fright, wondering if he would try to get in my bedroom window. I was too terrified to tell his wife as I knew that she would not believe me. For the first time in my mind I wanted to leave. I felt unsafe and insecure. I wanted to leave but because of my age I didn't. I did not have contact with any of my family, my uncles, my cousins, my father, my aunties, and my brothers and sisters at the time. Because of the Protectors and Sister McKenzie, I had no one to contact. How would anybody know what I was going through? Where is the guiding hand a child is meant to have?

He tried to get me down to the dairy shed. Can I show my anger as I write this? Fuck! I was alone. I felt sadness. I felt shame. I was hurting. The so called lay minister was only interested in his own personal sick gestures. One of my chores was to feed the chooks. I was constantly confronted with him exposing himself and masturbating. I ran from the chook shed dropping the bucket, this man with his erect penis violating my vulnerability. I was forced onto his marital bed with his hands mauling me. The torturing continued at my bedroom window telling me how to masturbate. I have a clear vision of this man who made suggestions at my bedroom window requesting that I should 'lie flat on your stomach and let your nipples rub onto the sheet'. I froze in my bed feeling angry and frightened. This is my body, my temple. Am I about to be destroyed? This continued for a long period and my innocence was eventually violated. I had lost all my pride. My God! Are these people God's People?

Since leaving Colebrook I had felt so insecure and isolated. My family was out there but I had no indication where they were. Were they searching for me? I needed to find out who my family was because I wanted them so desperately.

I felt these terrible experiences had ruined my life. I had lost all my dignity, self respect and, most importantly, my identity and sanity. I was isolated in a valley which swallowed me up. I can see myself standing there alone with no one to relate to, no one to help and comfort me. I wanted someone to come and take away the darkness.

Eventually, my sister Connie came to see me at this place. But I did not know how to approach her. I was just numb for the words to tell. I was reaching out to her for help but she was a stranger to me and I could not explain to her what had been happening. I was shamed. How could I tell anyone I needed to leave this place and why? This experience remained a bad secret until late in my adult years. These people were 'Christians' and I was placed in their care and trust by the United Aboriginal Mission. Later, I found out that another Colebrook girl went to that same farm after I'd left. She was abused just as I had been.

These incidents have played a major part in destroying my life. At this house, I was deprived of the normal happiness and bonding with other teenagers. Sharing the joys of going to outings or the pleasure of going to the pictures. I felt pretty isolated but I continued on with dignity. I really had no dreams or plans in life. The saddest thing is that I really didn't have a mum or family to guide me.

DREAMS

Walking through a blue dream,
Reality calls but it's not what it seems.
Living while the subconscious screams.
Living to find out what it all means.

Sometime before my sixteenth birthday, once again I was removed. I had no notion where I was going and there was no discussion about what was planned for me. All I knew was that I was leaving this dreadful place. I remember thinking that this man was running scared for what he did to me. It was obvious to me that he was only protecting himself. I was taken by this man of God from Coromandel Valley to work in a nursing home at Malvern in the city. The move to the nursing home was a form of escape for me.

I was dropped off with my small possessions at the nursing home expecting to start work immediately as a domestic and that's what happened. I enjoyed the work even though it was only in the kitchen. I made friends easily and I felt comfortable both with the staff and the residents. It gave me a sense of independence plus I was receiving regular wages. After settling in my new job and familiarising myself both with the nursing home and the area, I started to go out, feeling quite confident. I really enjoyed meeting the *marus* at the Saturday night dances at the Royal Palais in Adelaide.

On one occasion at the nursing home, a staff nurse came to me to let me know that I had a visitor. I walked to the front of the nursing home and found my older sister Doreen, waiting patiently, and proudly breast feeding her baby. I was really shamed. I approached her shyly. I knew she was my sister but we were like strangers. In a quiet voice I said something to her about feeding the baby in a public place. Doreen soon made it known to me quite boldly that it was okay to breast feed her baby openly. It was a brave stand for any woman to make back in the fifties. The visit was brief and pleasant but I still had the sense of not belonging. Here was this beautiful dignified small lady who had obviously searched for me. What made it worse was that the nursing sister suggested that I should not have any contact with my family or visitors. It was a Methodist Nursing Home. I have often wondered why she said this. Was it because of her ignorance? I needed my family. I had little contact with them. I did not know how to approach them as a member of a family should.

Having this job gave me much pleasure and also the ability to communicate both with the nursing staff and residents. On paydays I went with a friend who also worked at the nursing home, and wastefully spent my wage going to the pictures. I just had no idea of the value of money so I never saved, didn't really know how to. I didn't even have a bankbook. I was not interested in buying a car or flash clothes. I just did not have any goals in life, nor dreams, nor direction. I was just drifting. I wasn't taught the basics and I blissfully spent all the money I earned.

If I had some money left over I caught the train to Colebrook. I used to visit a few of the kids who were still at the home. I would be dressed with high heel shoes and stockings, feeling quite flash and wonderful as I had a job and a little money. I recall a time when I visited Colebrook with Christina Pinkie, another girl from the home who I regarded as my older sister and who was working as a domestic on a farm. She had already started the habit of smoking. While we were waiting for our brothers and sisters to join us, Christina lit up a smoke. We looked with surprise as the Superintendent told her to leave or put her smoke out. This man, Mr. Samuels, was blind but he certainly picked up the cigarette odour! Christina reluctantly put the smoke out—after a few giggles.

I was pretty close to Christina. I recall the times at Colebrook when she teased the hell out of me.

Christina had the habit of calling me by my nickname, Canary, and ripping my pants up the cheeks of my backside. I immediately cried and ran to Sister Hyde followed by Christina calling me a sooky baby. I met up with Christina years later at the dances when we both worked at Northfield Hospital. We reminisced about Colebrook. We had lost a few years but found each other.

Need to Belong

Being brought up as a strict Christian, I found it hard to express my personal feelings and had a great need to belong to someone. I had left Colebrook with a lot of disillusionment because of the continual sexual harassment put upon me at an early age by a member of the staff and then later with the lay preacher. These were horrendous experiences which caused me great confusion in my teens. I never really had a boyfriend but I was working and playing sport. Eventually I met a man with whom I had two children. Things were not going too good for us. We moved houses many times with little furniture. Food was scarce. I recall having no refrigerator at one place and I tried to set jelly in the coolest place in the house. In the end the relationship became sour. I remember leaving the father of the children, with my belongings packed in glad bags, no bloody cases, just these green plastic bags. I hustled the children and our small belongings, pots and pans, into a taxi to take us to my sister Christina's place. We stayed with her until I was able to find a flat.

Then, after all my changes of moving houses, I did meet someone whom I married. I had another child. In those days it was the proper thing to get married. I wanted this marriage more for the stability of my children's upbringing than for myself. That marriage didn't work and we divorced. To me, marriage wasn't meant for me! It took me many years to work through my emotions. I was constantly looking for security. I had it with my children, watching them grow in the times of hardship and the years of struggle. My relationship with the fathers of the children was not exceedingly compatible! Since I received little money from the welfare and no help or financial assistance from either of the fathers, supporting my children as the breadwinner has strengthened me. My children didn't have a father figure so there were difficult times for me. I continued being a single parent on the pension, or finding work where possible. As a sole parent back in the sixties there wasn't much government assistance.

The struggling continued as we moved house many times. I recall having Christmas lunch with my friends Christina and Tom. The house was run down and I didn't have much furniture. I begin to grin as I write. The table wasn't steady, the chairs were rickety, other seats were just kero drums. Yet the meal was prepared in such a way that I can almost taste the succulent turkey even now as I continue my writing with a small giggle.

I needed to search for my people. My first contact with Aboriginals was when I travelled on the train to Adelaide station when I was still living at Colebrook Home as a child. This was a new experience for me and the other kids and we anxiously looked around at the Adelaide Station. This was the *maru* meeting place and seeing them gave us great joy.

The Carrington Hotel was such a place—a meeting place for the Aboriginals and a pick-up joint for the white fellas. A place for telling jokes, laughing, getting drunk, and telling yarns. I recall the days when I played hockey for a competitive team, the Inlanders, with my sister Avis. It was a game that we both enjoyed. We went to the Carrington after the games and met up with other Aboriginal people. The place buzzed with high vitality. It was run down, with little furniture, no table and chairs, just cold hard benches in the main bar. The whole place stank of stale beer and cigarette smoke, a smell that lingered at the entrance of the pub. The strong odour of disinfectant made it worse. At nights the place was bursting at the seams with the laughter of people and the drawn out Ngarrindjeri lingo. The atmosphere had warmth.

The nights changed as things became louder and more boisterous during the course of the evening. The publicans made their money and the people became intoxicated. Then of course came the unnecessary arrests by the police. Avis and I were young with young families. Our hope was to meet up with our relations at the hotel, many of whom we had never met. It was a real culture shock. We were going to have a good time and meet the people who were regulars at the hotel. I found nothing wrong with people enjoying themselves. The atmosphere was high with energy. Everyone was slightly inebriated and merry.

I remember when I was picked up for a minor offence. I became a bit loud and boisterous and began to swear. I was soon in the paddy van with other dis-orderly drunks. I was scared, being held in this cold van and taken to the Adelaide police station to be interviewed by a female officer. One thing that stayed in my mind was the officer who stroked my hair telling me that I had nice hair. I became wary and worried, as I had never been in trouble with the law. I was soon on my merry way. I was free and no charges were laid.

The night air was crisp and cold as I stepped outside the station. I remember going home in the early hours of the morning feeling sorry for myself. I decided then that this would never happen again. I was shamed. This experience made me think twice and I have never been in contact with the law again.

Even today I quite often think of all the un-necessary effort that the police expended on the many Aboriginals who always seemed to be happy and quite harmless. The Carrington Hotel was reaping the profits. The publican encouraged the patrons to become drunk and rowdy. If things got out of hand the police were called in. These occurrences happened frequently, mainly on pension days or the weekends. It wasn't uncommon to see a police car patrolling outside the pub.

Everyone had a purpose to meet at this place. For me it was an opportunity to reach out to my family. At this time I was doing a lot of soul searching and getting to know who I was and who they were. On leaving Colebrook, I hadn't realised that there was a large family circle to meet. By going to the hotel, it helped me to meet a large number of my aunts, uncles and cousins. Being exposed to this sort of environment gave me a sense of belonging.

Around about this time in the seventies, after the breakdown of my marriage, I decided to get out of Adelaide. I sold most of my furniture and had my heart set on living in Western Australia. I was all packed and sitting on my suitcases when my closest friend, Margaret, came into the house.

'What's all this?'

'I'm going to Western Australia to live.'

'You're not going there, *kungka*[9]. You're coming to Raukkan with me!'

My cousin, Sandra, was standing amongst the confusion. 'I'll buy your kitchen cupboard,' she said.

Margaret and her husband Paul lived at Raukkan in a small stone house which was cool on hot days. Their house was overcrowded but we coped. This was the first time that I had ever been to Raukkan since I was a few weeks old and stolen from my family. I found it a beautiful place with the lake in front and the old church on the hill. That church is on the fifty-dollar note now.

Our stay was brief. The children settled in well. They kept themselves busy hunting for rabbits. I lay in bed in the early hours of the morning hearing the

9 kungka: woman

kids coming home to skin the rabbits and gut them in the small kitchen. Then I'd hear one of the kids, 'Uncle Paul this one has kittens'. My kids went to the Raukkan school. They had a few fights because the kids there might have thought they were white fellas. They were different. There was a lot of excitement and activity there. Leisure time was when we went fishing. We did a lot of fishing. We went to the Coorong, just lazing around on the beach. I was meeting many of my relations. It was fun the way they spoke, some of them with a very drawn out accent. They made me crack up laughing. I loved their free spirit.

Totti was Margaret's cousin. She was a large woman, with her humour and drawn out lingo. I loved her and all her family. I found the people were very high spirited—plenty of laughter, not like the people in Adelaide.

There was alcohol abuse though, and I had to adjust to that, which was the hardest thing to do. I wasn't used to seeing drunks falling all over the place. There were lots of times when fellas were drunk and falling around. How it affected me was that I was scared. It was frightening but I managed to cope with it because of my experiences living in Adelaide.

Down there you have got the open space, the fresh air and you are on Ngarrindjeri land. But it was very hard for me to fit into the community, and to find my own people. I think the lingo was the most difficult part for me to learn. I was laughed at when I came out with the wrong words or when I pronounced some words wrong. I still today don't know how to say 'police' in the Ngarrindjeri language. I have since learnt some of the language and teach it, including the Pitjantjatjara language, to my grandchildren. Our language was lost but it has been revived.

I eventually moved to Murray Bridge when a house became available, and it was even harder there. We lived in several houses until the Nungas Housing Committee offered a Tudor house with bay windows. This last house was huge with a big backyard. I planted native trees and settled comfortably. I enjoyed the spacious rooms and, in particular, the open fire and the old wood stove. This was my home and I furnished it for our comfort. The children were happy and attended the local schools. At the end of the street were the Nungas' flats for the elders.

As a mother, I had a lot of adjustments to deal with in Murray Bridge. This was a testing and trying time for me. I got numerous jobs to support my family. I used to work at the local Clipsal factory and during fruit picking season I'd go out picking grapes. My worst job experience was picking peas. My niece,

Rosslyn, and I had to start working at six in the morning. We were in so much agony we literally crawled along the ground throughout the day and by the end of the day our bodies were aching. It was bloody hard work and we only lasted one day. There was no way we were ever going back.

I enjoyed cooking and my culinary abilities were soon put to the test when my older sister, Connie, approached me to make her daughter's wedding cake. I was a bit skeptical of my ability but agreed jokingly to make a three-tier cake. The making of the cake was a challenge and very time consuming but I gained a lot of pleasure from it. I had no proper utensils, measuring cups or scales and completed the project by guesswork. Word spread and my cake-making skills were soon in great demand. From then on I began to use my expertise in wedding cakes for the Aboriginal community. I was being productive and assertive in what I was doing for my people.

I did office cleaning and I also worked at the Regional Education Office which I found uninteresting. One day as I was working at the office, Gwenda, who also worked at Murray Bridge came to tell me the news of my father's death. I had no emotions and couldn't cry. The emptiness I felt left me hollow. I really never got to know my father. He was buried at

Raukkan, Point McLeay. At the funeral I found it difficult to shed a tear. I remember Jennadene saying, 'It's okay to cry Mum,' but I couldn't.

I continued to live in Murray Bridge and subsequently got a job for two years as a secretary at the Lower Murray Nungas Club. This was in 1983 and my cousin Aileen Wilson employed me. I was actively involved with the Nunga Housing Committee, the *Wama*[10] programme and on many other committees.

It was difficult for me to fit in with the Aboriginal community. I had to find out who was related to me and this was frustrating. All of a sudden I found out what a huge extended family I belonged to. Aunties, uncles, cousins, all over the place. It was very difficult to know them all. I needed to familiarise myself with the local Nunga language. This created much amusement in the local community as I tried to express myself with the lingo.

The difficulty of relating to my people was a great hurdle for me. I found myself in a position where I had to get used to the negative attitude amongst the Aboriginal community. The past always seemed to be brought up and they always had the habit of putting people down. This was a big problem but everyone seemed to adjust to it. I became frustrated, as I had to

---

10 wama: alcohol

accept criticism because I spoke differently or acted differently. I was treated as an outsider. The social problems with drink had a horrendous effect on me. At this time I drank quite excessively to overcome my frustration within the town. I survived the ridicule and the shame but I became unwell.

My father Oswald Kartinyeri (deceased).

JOURNEYS FROM REALITY

THE GREAT GARDENS OF MONATO

I had my first acute episode of mental illness back in 1984 when I was living in Murray Bridge. I had travelled by bus to visit a friend in Adelaide. I had been invited to stay but when I arrived at the house, my friend wasn't in sight. I made myself at home. After settling in, I decided to go to the nearest park. Away from the bustling traffic, I had great intentions to do a wonderful sketch with the few implements in my possession. My lead pencil and sketch book were the only tools I had—my weapons. I sat in a most secluded area admiring the beautiful surroundings. I sat cross-legged, drawing this most 'wonderful' tree in this 'wonderful' park. I was feeling 'wonderful,' not realising that I was sick. The effort that I put into the drawing wasn't successful. I was in harmony with Mother Nature, absorbing the stillness and the tranquillity. I spent about an hour in this space. I was trapped inside my own world. I closed myself away from reality. It was an escape, my escape! It was wonderful. I wandered back to the house. I was in my own little world, completely unaware of what was going on around me. I never got to see my friend. I have no recollection of what followed.

On another occasion while watching television, I almost killed my nephew, Robert, with a piece of firewood I raised in the air. Robert and his cousins were watching a video, something like *Planet of the Apes*. My journey in the ambulance to Glenside was a trip I will never forget. I distinctly remember Jennadene travelling with me, talking to me and comforting me. At times I moved from side to side, in motion with the ambulance as it travelled through the hills. I persisted in giving the ambulance attendants the directions. My mind was wide awake and things were intensely crystal clear. Eventually my body relaxed completely and I pissed myself in the ambulance before getting to Glenside Hospital.

While waiting for the doctor, I was making strange *ooh* sounds. I was reading the eye chart, A E I O U, as I lay restlessly on the hard bed. I was boisterous and vocal. I had visions of my son going blind. Eventually Dr. Thompson arrived. I supposedly said aloud, 'About time, Thomo.' He had no choice but to admit me to the hospital. My stay at Glenside was tormenting and long. I was heavily medicated, being subjected to numerous forms of different medications. I was like a zombie, and my whole body was disjointed. My head felt all twisted around to one side. It was a terrible feeling—that stiffness in my neck, and not knowing what was happening to me. The alienation was awful. There was no one there for me. The hospital was huge and noisy, with no privacy and the continuous disruption of other patients.

Glenside had beautiful grounds, but the inside of the wards were morbid and dingy. In my zombie state of mind I wandered around in the grounds, among the tall gum trees and smaller shrubs, aimlessly. Inside, I felt trapped.

There were times that I thought I would die. I dreaded each day. I had no sense of self-esteem and no incentive or motivation to do any kind of work about the house. I woke up in the mornings, wandered aimlessly to the kitchen and forced myself to prepare breakfast. Doing the dishes and the housework was a big task. It was even a huge effort to bath myself. My visits to the doctors helped me from time to time. But the cycle always began again. I returned home from the hospital each time overcome with mixed feelings of isolation and loneliness. I had no interest in reading. It was a huge task to comprehend my surroundings.

Many years later, I was told that I suffer from Bi-Polar Affective Disorder or manic-depression. My illness has been something that I have had to struggle very hard to come to terms with. My illness constantly fluctuates between extreme highs and extreme lows. To go through manic-depression is pure hell. Like maggots, this condition was destroying me slowly by eating away at my body, mind and soul.

With my mood swings, I have been through many trials and tribulations. A huge part of my life has been on hold due to my illness. When I become manic, my mind becomes extremely active and travels at the most extraordinary pace. Things happen too quickly for me. The journey that I experience can be beautiful but my visions can also be mangled with many shocking results. They are so real that I can't believe I am hallucinating. The whole world is elevated to such speed that I can see myself picking flowers in the fields. These beautiful journeys that I am travelling in, I would not wish on anybody.

I recall going for a walk one day in the paddocks of Monato, picking flowers and feeling extremely 'wonderful'. My beautiful bunch of flowers turned out to be a handful of weeds. My son was with me at the time. I had driven the car to the 'great gardens' of

Monato and then on to my best friend's place with these horrible looking weeds. The day continued with me doing very weird things. I had a bizarre set of hallucinations. My whole body felt as if it had been taken over. I was seeing faces appearing through my bedroom window, faces that I knew. I had built up an excess of energy and was drinking a lot of water. Things had really speeded up, like a video going on fast forward. By evening I was exhausted. In the early hours of the morning, things started to get out of hand. Everything was moving too fast for me. I just was not in control of my mind, body or soul. My children, nephew and my best friend, Margaret, had a great time chasing me through the house and in and out of windows. Even the ambulance officers chased me down the street in the early hours of the morning. Nobody could find me. I was cunning. I was lying flat on my back in the ambulance ready to be transported to the hospital.

The most bizarre episode during my illness was an occasion when I demonstrated in my yard, in a dignified manner, that I was a full blood Aboriginal lady walking with my dog, hunting and searching for a lost baby. I was stark naked. I sat on the front lawn and I could see myself sitting cross-legged and communicating with a group of traditional people. My pet dog, that was supposedly a dingo, accompanied me as I walked proudly around the house stark naked, wearing only the hat that Eva Johnson, the playwright, had given to me. I still have that hat hanging in my bedroom.

During another psychotic episode, my local doctor had to chase me around the house to give me an injection in the *mana*. This day was a busy day for my sister Margaret who was extremely exhausted by the end. As my moods swung, my behaviour changed dramatically. I became almighty active and truly wound up. The adrenalin inside me was overwhelming. As I ran through the house, I suddenly noticed a spool of speaker wire lying on the passage floor and thought immediately that I was being filmed. Running past it, I felt wonderfully high. I thought a documentary was being made of me. I ran through the hallway, *nukkin*[11] at the reel of speaker wire on the floor, then raced to my bedroom. I felt like a butterfly, flitting from room to room. Eventually I twisted myself up in the bedding. Feeling suffocated, I moved swiftly out of bed and found myself curled up with a pillow on the cold floor next to the toilet bowl. Poor Margaret! God knows where I would have been if it

---

11 nukkin: looking

wasn't for her. Margaret came and rescued me but I also tired her as she tried to keep up with my erratic pace. She was always there for me. She was extremely tolerant and compassionate, and quite amused by my bizarre movements throughout the house.

From time to time I visited my family in Murray Bridge. On one occasion I had become rather manic again. My daughter Jennadene was in full control and drove me to the local doctor at the Bridge Clinic who seemed to have a funny name. This bothered me. We sat motionless in the waiting room. I was a little vocal but having Jennadene with me and feeling her presence, I felt at ease. I could feel her strength. My name was soon called. Jennadene's face as she quietly said, 'Mum, the doctor's ready' reassured me as she led me into the room. In my confused mind, I managed to hear the word 'Bi-Polar' being used by the doctor and Jennadene. On my way out I gave the doctor a quick hug, then referring to my illness, I said 'What, it came all the way from Poland?' and chuckled as I left the consulting room.

Another time, I stayed on at John and Jennifer's at Murray Bridge. I was sick. I see myself lying on a hard bed. I felt I was dying, fighting for my life. I was afraid to close my eyes. I fought for every breath. I lay with my hands across my chest, then suddenly, realising that I needed to change my position, I quickly moved my hands to my sides. I wrestled with the covers, fighting for my life. The adrenalin rushed through my body as I struggled to stay alive. Was it just a dream? Or was I hallucinating? Or was it real? I remember lying there tying myself in a knot, suffocating myself, entwining the sheets around me on that very hot day.

Then there was the time I was in the state of manic-depression. Jennadene was preparing me to go to hospital. Jennadene was tiring from my erratic movements as I became quite vocal. My mind was working brilliantly as I began to see things in a different perspective. I ran through the small passage out of the house, in a manic stage. I followed her to the bathroom and stood in a position of hopelessness watching the level of the shampoo as it was slowly rising in the bottle. 'Forever and ever, Amen. That's fucking enough. Forever, Amen!' I pronounced repeatedly.

Jennadene was trying to keep up with my athletic mind. I moved swiftly through the house yelling, 'Forever, Amen!' I chimed the small bell in the lounge room devoutly yelling, 'Forever, Amen. Forever, Amen!' My illness started to have an immense effect, not only on me but also on my family. I was finally sent away in a government car. John rang and was told by Jennadene that I was in the government car being transported to Woodleigh House. John replied, 'Poor Mum still being taken by the government.'

BROKEN SPIRIT

I search for my soul
I search for my heart
my spirit is broken the white fella's way
I journey into a world of confusion
travelling deep into my thoughts
my journey is dark with no opening
my cries are not heard
I look into my soul's emptiness

I'm in tune with my surroundings
on the Ngarrindjerri land
my spirit is not broken
I fight, I survive

My illness is controlled by medication. There are times when I was fine, then the medication slowed me down or made me become a little agitated. When I visited my sister Avis, I was so unwell that I was up and down from the chair or the bed like a yo-yo. Avis was supportive. She kept telling me to relax. After a while this behaviour was so frustrating, for me and for Avis, she had to ring the Aboriginal Health to take me to the hospital.

There were times I felt I didn't exist. I just drifted. This was distressing for me. I wanted to be normal. The buses passed my place as I lay on my bed, gazing into space, thinking of nothing. I slept long hours. The days were long with no visitors, no health workers or support from other organisations. I couldn't wait for night to come so I could escape from the world. During the long days and nights, I silently shuffled many miles around the house in despair. Wishing I was able to laugh and joke. I could hear myself shuffling around the house trying to function like everybody else. Trying to adjust to what was happening around me.

My days usually began with me questioning, 'What's ahead of me?' Nothing seemed productive. I had no plans or ambition. I had to fight to survive and hope things would be better the following day. I'd look around the house feeling useless and empty. My mind was a vacuum. I admired the family photos that sat on the sideboard and began to cry.

I gather myself together, then light a cigarette. My habit has increased immensely. I step outside to drive to the shop to buy a packet of cigarettes. The world is buzzing.

This is the real world so I move swiftly, but I drive cautiously, aware of what surrounds me. I sit in despair at the traffic lights. Time is racing but not to my pace.

I have struggled over the years due to my illness. I became quite erratic and tended to overspend my money, or commit myself to bigger debts, signing my life away. When I was ill no one was around to see if I was okay. I seemed to be in control, not knowing that I was overspending or unwell. I did these irrational things in a psychosis or manic disorder, feeling really 'wonderful' about the products I had just bought. It's just my illness, overspending! At least I am not running around starkers doing the shopping.

I have inflicted injuries on myself by trying to end my life on many occasions. I've overdosed and even tried to kill myself in my car on the freeway. My loneliness caused a problem with alcohol abuse. It becomes painful as I relive the past, which will always be a part of me, but I try not to let it control me. Life must go on.

My sisters tried to encourage me by saying, '*Kungka* come on, be strong.' Yes, I should. I must fight this depression and think only of the positive but it was hard to do it alone. Where is everybody?

Jennadene, my eldest daughter, was always helpful and compassionate but she was not coping, so she admitted me to Glenside. I stayed a short period and was transferred to Woodleigh House, a psychiatric hospital nearer to my home. I felt uncomfortable within myself but had no choice about it.

No sooner had I arrived at Woodleigh House than I was queuing up for my medication. At times, walking aimlessly through the wards of the hospital, I was filled with feelings of hopelessness and worthlessness. There were times I felt like a guinea pig being pumped full of medications. Some of the medications made me feel ill. I distinctly remember the side effects of one in particular. My whole body was affected and I walked with stiffness in my muscles. I had great difficulties in moving my neck and my whole body ached. Come mealtime I had trouble eating, then I'd vomit. I had no control over my well-being. The thing is, I had no say. I was administered these pills. 'Medication time,' the nurse called!

I was detained for twenty-one days, so I really had no bloody choice in what was happening to my mind, body and soul. I had highs and lows and my memories were vague so then I began to lose or misplace items.

I became frustrated as I searched for them but to no avail.

I was put on doses of thioridazine so that my thoughts slowed down, and I functioned in a manner that I seemed out of control. The laughter had gone. God! I am human. I have the right to function, expressing emotions that may have offended people. I feel. I hurt. I'm fucking normal. What right does anyone have to pump me with these monstrous medications, pills that make me escape from reality? Without my spirit I'm non-existent. I need my spirit to be whole. I need my spirit to give me strength to survive in the tangled mess of society.

This idea of writing this book came to me while I was ill in hospital. I wanted to pass down to my children the experiences I had in Colebrook Home. I repeatedly said to Jennadene, 'I'm going to write a book one day.' I never dreamt that it could happen. It just never entered my mind, until I became ill again. Frequently, I said to Jennadene 'Well this is chapter one or two.' Jennadene just replied, 'Yes, Mum' or 'alright, Mum' or 'You do it, Mum.' I wanted to put pen to paper telling my experiences of being stolen from my family, of hardships, of adolescence and coping without parental guidance and the difficulties of dealing with my illness. I sat in isolation in a large cold room in another institution and I began to scribble the words that made sense to me.

As my visions became stronger, I became erratic. My mind raced again. I called aloud, 'End of chapter! End of book! End of chapter! End of book! End of book! End of chapter!' I sat at the computer with my daughter-in-law. 'End of chapter! Praise the Lord, Amen! Praise the Lord, Amen!' Then I was taken to hospital, Woodleigh House. The ward was full of dynamic patients. Everyone was scurrying around. Do I feel safe in this confusion? My writing became irregular as I sat motionless in these chaotic surroundings. Then it was put on hold for months.

In the hospital, I had feelings of isolation and having no contact with anybody. In this time an old hymn came to my mind. 'Give me oil in my lamp keep me burning, give me oil in my lamp I pray!' The Bible stories and songs calmed my thoughts as I wandered up to my room to rock myself to sleep, a habit that I developed as a child.

On one particular day while I was in Woodleigh House, I was woken up by a member of the staff and told that I had two interesting 'flowery' visitors. I immediately flew off my bed knowing that it was my nephew Robert and his girlfriend Kerry. These two beautiful people were waiting downstairs, Robert clutching a large bunch of wild flowers which looked as though he had just stripped them nearby. We stood in a circle and embraced. I guessed a visit from Robert and Kerry impressed my doctor.

Robert had put the flowers in a bright yellow vase, which was exceedingly appropriate, and placed them right under the doctor's nose. The aroma from the flowers was intensely strong and I spoke quietly to Robert suggesting the smell of the flowers was just a bit too strong. 'It's alright Auntie,' he said as we sat and talked with the doctor. Robert and Kerry were both firing questions at him. The visit was meant to happen. Here I was a sleeping patient and then suddenly rescued and swept away by two beautiful people. They took me home!

My first experience with any psychiatrist was when I was living at Murray Bridge. I had to travel to and from Adelaide to visit the psychiatrist, not knowing what was expected of me and how to deal with the problems I had. What would it be like to have my mind examined by a stranger? I had no one with me on my visits to the psychiatrists but then again I appreciated my time out. In this tiny room I sat looking, motion-less, not feeling agitated. I took time out to study the doctor, thinking how much this doctor reminded of Woody Allen as he scribbled my family tree on a large pad. I would be *nukkin* at this *tjilpi*[12] in a sly manner thinking that he was *cutta*[13] not me. I was never comfortable with this man. But I guess he was doing his job even though I can say honestly that I didn't have a clue what was happening to me. On leaving the clinic I had even more feelings of isolation. No one to turn to, to talk with or to joke about what I had just been through.

Once again, I was referred to another doctor in the same surgery. These two doctors reminded me of the Bible story of David and Goliath. Here I was confronted with this huge man. I felt really scared and I knew that these visits were only a waste of time. As I didn't comprehend any discussion or so called counselling, I just sat staring. I can recall that there wasn't too much discussion anyway. I sat in silence— you could hear a pin drop. I felt helpless and couldn't wait to walk swiftly out from the clinic, feeling quite disillusioned and more confused than ever.

I have experienced emotional manipulation. I think it is wrong to manipulate others and poison their minds with words and actions that make them feel

---

12 tjilpi: old man
13 cutta: silly

bad. Manipulation can occur at many different levels. People in authority like to have full control, which makes others feel vulnerable. As a child in Colebrook Home, there were authority figures who took advantage of me emotionally. My whole life has been moulded into a statue without liberty. My movements were restricted as a child and they felt restricted now. It frightens me to think there are people out there who are heartless and lacking the intelligence to know that they can affect people so deeply that it carries on throughout their life.

After leaving Murray Bridge and moving to Adelaide I have had repeated episodes of my mental illness and spent a lot of time in hospital. I struck another psychiatrist, who I didn't feel comfortable with at first. On meeting Dr. Kenny through my social worker I just had to chuckle to myself as I found her Christian name extremely amusing, sounding *pilyki*[14] but I'm not sure if Dr. Kenny saw the funny side of it. To me, then, she was only another therapist who was going to try to examine this black brain.

She always seemed serious and looked a toffee little sophisticated *kungka* wearing her hair up in a French roll. There were many times that I would

---

14 pilyki: dirty

nukkin through Dr. Kenny, questioning myself why this little *kungka* all the way from another country, Scotland, was trying to see through me. How was she going to get inside this *maru* head when she didn't know the Aboriginal culture that was stolen from me? I said to myself that no one would understand me or get through this little *maru* brain.

There were times that I would *ngunti*[15] but I'm sure Dr Kenny knew exactly what was going on in my head. Our sessions continued on and, for the first time, I had finally met a doctor who I felt comfortable with and who was comfortable with me. There were still some times that I felt a little uncomfortable as I thought she was helpful but I'd chuckle to myself thinking, God I wish this *kungka* would speak bloody English. I found her Scottish accent a bit frustrating and hard to comprehend and I mimiced her accent mockingly aloud or under my breath.

I have received professional counselling and help from Dr. Kenny over a period of four years so I do have a lot of confidence in her. And we have an under-standing and continue to relate in a more rational manner today. I think in a way, that I have also been helpful to her as well. Today I like to think that things

---

15 ngunti: lie

are going well for me now. If I need any further counselling, I know that Dr. Kenny will always be there. I regard Dr. Kenny as a friend and as a professional person who has played an important part in my life. I appreciate her credibility and her trust. Thank you Dr. Kenny.

I was fortunate to have a local GP who always had time to listen. Dr. Kate always asked me how 'wonderful' I felt. On my arrival at her surgery room I often sat motionless feeling quite untroubled. If I was on a normal high, I was well. If I was too 'wonderful', then I was sick.

OH, WHAT A FEELING!

My doors have always been open for my people, my brothers and sisters from Colebrook. I entertained my regular visitors with parties and alcohol. I found time to listen and to laugh with them. I think the saddest thing was no contact with people when I became ill. I received no counselling or visits from the Aboriginal Health. There was little support or understanding from many of my friends. No one wanted to take the time to understand. I still have had no follow up visits from the Aboriginal Health. I scarcely used the phone. I felt isolated. I believe this was due to ignorance and that people were wary of mental illness.

When I was on a natural high, people continuously asked me if I was alright. This bothered me. How the bloody hell am I suppose to feel? There are a lot of erratic people out there. Am I always the one they notice? My friends and family asked, 'Have you taken your medication?' or 'Medication time?' The sound of these words ring in my ear. Of course, I have indeed answered their questioning but sometimes wondered who was sick. I realise that my friends were concerned about me. But I was okay and I knew I was in control and that I was someone special. I was close to my spirituality and close to my land.

The day Jennadene and Tanya came to visit me in hospital will always be a memory that stays with me. I was playing table tennis when the two girls headed my way. I looked with amazement and jumped with excitement, 'Oh what a feeling, my daughters!'

I often visited Jennadene and my grandchildren at Murray Bridge. I sat and talked. My mind flowed as I spent an immense time reasoning about my illness. Jennadene listened, taking notice of my movements and feeling sympathetic. She has always had a gentle nature. I remember saying to her, 'The world is weird' then I quickly corrected myself. 'It's not the world. It's those who control it.' Jennadene swiftly replied, 'Insanity is the safest place to be, Mum.'

Moving to Adelaide gave me greater employment opportunities. I saw an advertisement in the *Advertiser* looking for Aboriginal people interested in Enrolled Nursing. I applied and was successful. I was overwhelmed to be chosen for the one-year course to be conducted at Queen Elizabeth Hospital. The group was diverse in age and background. This did not stop me from having a great time and sharing many laughs in the classroom. The Director of Nursing was understanding and tolerant towards us. The course gave me confidence and pride in myself. Unfortunately, I had to leave after nine months to look after myself and my mental state.

Bellara is a nursing home where I worked for four years. Bellara is an Aboriginal name. It was a good job and I enjoyed my time there as a nursing assistant. The staff were excellent and I made friends with the staff, the residents and the relatives of the residents. I travelled to work on a scooter. I had not yet bought a car, and I enjoyed the freedom of avoiding the busy traffic. I had no licence and was unaware that I needed one. One night I was suddenly confronted by the law.

It was the police setting up the breathalyser. Fortunately I had just completed an evening shift and was still in uniform. Although I did panic, I was soon ushered on by the boys in blue. I continued riding my scooter until I bought a car from one of the girls from the nursing home. I found out later that I needed a licence for the scooter. But I was never caught.

I enjoyed my stay at Bellara. In the four years I worked there, I received many memorable challenges until unfortunately I became ill again. I appreciated the concern of my mates. Most of the staff knew when I became sick and that I would have to be admitted to Hillcrest Hospital.

I remember a time when I was at my son's place on a high, feeling over 'wonderful'. I was being loud and cheerful. I had this need to go to Bellara even though I wasn't on duty. I arrived on the doorstep of the home. Cally, my niece, was in the car waiting for me. My mind and body was in an athletic state. I was feeling confident. I felt it was important for me to be there.

I now ask the question, who was guiding me? Somebody was with me because I had no memory of getting to my destination. I was walking through the nursing home *tjina nikiti*[16]. I checked on the patients

---

16 tjina nikiti: bare foot

as I passed through the corridors, floating through the wards like a guardian angel. My favourite senior staff member, Marilyn, was on duty, and she was able to recognise that I was not well and that something was wrong.

Fortunately my mate Colleen was also on duty. Colleen had made coffee so we sat and talked for a while. Soon after we had spoken I was on my way back doing the rounds of the wards. I felt like a bird flying freely in and out of the building caring for my patients. Colleen was with me watching over all my movements. I ran out to the back of the nursing home, wandering aimlessly down the alleyway back to the car where my niece was waiting patiently. I was watching over the patients in my special way. I cared about the people in the home. I'm not a religious person but I do believe that someone had been watching over me. Then blow me down the same night I got pulled over by the breathalyser. I was on a high but it was not through alcohol so I passed and my high wasn't detected, thank God!

In the past I have experimented with marijuana to calm my manic state. However I know now that *yardi* is bad for mental illness. Or is it? But it did give me a real buzz! I had two beautiful plants growing along my side fence. One night one of my sisters was with me and she said, 'Check the *yardi* plants. They must be ready to pick.' We went out and the smell of the plants was strong. 'Leave them for a couple of days,' I said. Next morning, I noticed a trail of dirt across the lawn and the plants were gone. I blamed the dog. I thought she had got into the pot plants. Then I realised it was the neighbours. I flew around in an angry mood. Of course they denied it but I heard them snipping away the buds as I arrived. Now I'm *nukkin* at a deadly answering machine. They gave it to me out of guilt!

MY GUIDING HANDS

Being diagnosed as a sufferer of Bi-Polar Affective Disorder and learning to come to terms with it after many years of frustration and loneliness, I would like to share the journey of visions and rituals that I experienced. Being brought up with religion and having my own belief, I continued on living with a strong spiritual force. I have experienced many un-explained occurrences in my life.

One night I remember keeping my children and family awake all night with great urges to drink glass after glass of water. I continually wandered back and forward from my bedroom to the kit-chen drinking furiously and feeling 'wonderful'. I climbed back into bed. I became restless and, while lying on the bed, I saw a vision of a foetus appearing on the face of the clock radio. I looked at it aimlessly. Every time I looked at the clock-face it was there staring back at me. This painful vision continued throughout the night. Later I rose from my bed. Turning to the window,

I saw faces appearing, people I know who cared about me. They were staring through the glass. I was motionless. I had feelings of deep sadness but I didn't know what it was about.

I now believe that this represented the foetus of my unborn child. I had a relationship with a white man I met who worked for the Department of Aboriginal Affairs. My children didn't like this man. They made fun of him whenever he went off his head with rage. I fell pregnant to him and I was soon pressured by him to have an abortion. It was a relationship that I was never happy in and it should not have happened. He shouted and raved with anger like a mad man, 'Get rid of that baby! This will ruin my reputation!' I had the abortion, feeling a sigh of relief along with the pain. I received no counselling in the hospital. I was isolated as I had to travel alone from Murray Bridge to the maternity ward in Adelaide. It amazes me how some fucking white men can use black women.

One time, visiting Murray Bridge, my hometown, I was once again both heavenly and emotionally involved with a sweet and wonderful event. My daughter-in-law had just given birth to a beautiful son, baby Jacob. So I visited my son John, his wife Jennifer, the girls and baby Jacob. Being involved with the Hindmarsh Island issue, I became ill. Although feeling 'wonderful' I was not well. I was out on the front lawn playing 'Kick the Tin' with my granddaughters. At one stage I was getting quite aggressive with the tin, kicking it with all my might and cursing the white government for what they had done to me by taking me from my family. Unaware of what was happening to me I somehow managed to gather my five granddaughters in the early hours of the next morning, bathed them and then placed them all in the car and drove them to the hospital to see Jennifer and the new baby.

The amazing thing was that the children weren't belted up in the car and here I was being driven by some power with these precious little souls in the front and back seats of the car. I was singing, 'Jesus loves the little children, all the children of the world,' the tears streaming down my cheeks as I was singing. I had no idea what time it was or where I was. On arrival at the hospital, I sat my granddaughters in a circle, singing and passing baby Jacob to each of the girls in turn. He is precious and special. My mind and thoughts travelled rapidly doing these activities with my granddaughters who seemed to be quite happy joining in what I was doing. The fact is that it was meant to happen. It was a ritual journey with my granddaughters that we needed to make. I had given Jennifer a mother-of-pearl gift which an indigenous American Indian had given me, and it was for baby Jacob. I had rung the hospital extremely late the night before to inquire about Jennifer and the baby. On my arrival with the girls, Jennifer had gathered that I wasn't well and had to drive me home. It was only seven thirty in the morning. John was cursed by Jennifer on our arrival.

Once again I wasn't well. My eldest daughter Jennadene took me to the Murray Bridge Hospital to see the duty doctor. Feeling extremely 'wonderful' once again, I had previously picked flowers with two of my granddaughters. On arrival at the hospital, I clearly saw a white, cold, sterile bed and silently placed the flowers on the bed to form a cross. To me this was my mother's bed and it was an important ceremony which I had never before been able to experience. The image was crystal clear: the white sheets, the flowers, everything gleaming. It was a meaningful symbol for my soul, a sign of purity of connection, nothing was in the way between me and my Mother.

AUTUMN LEAVES

The autumn leaves have fallen
thickly carpeting the ground
the nights are cold.
Mother you have kept me warm
now you have gone.
The government has taken me away
the bond is shattered
the leaves have withered and died
I think of the times we shared together
and I will follow your dreams.

I have been inspired by many Aboriginal writers like Eva Johnson, Sally Morgan, and Jimmi Chi. Eva gave me a job as a prop woman for her play *Murra's*[17]. I watched Eva yelling at us, 'come on', as we giggled to ourselves on the set. Eva was tough. She was strong. She was loud and vibrant. She was dedicated to her work as a playwright. She was political. And her strength inspired me. A painting done by Eva is hanging in my lounge room.

The strength of these artists has inspired me in many ways. I am a survivor, one with a sense of pride

---

17 Murra's: Hands

and dignity. Looking back, it angers me now to think that the system of the so called bloody Aboriginal Protection Board and so called Christians had the power to remove Aboriginal children from their families and place them into Christian institutions. These institutions rammed Christian beliefs into children, brainwashing them into a system that stripped them of their people, their culture, their beliefs, their rules, their traditions. We had our own rules, our own ways of living. We had our own creation stories, our spirituality. What right did they have to crush our spirituality, our language, our kin? What right did they have to crush our spirit and replace it with their myths and stories and rules which they did not live up to. And which they used to violate our lives? The whole bloody system stank.

How dare they interfere with the integrity of Aboriginal families. Many families suffered emotionally and spiritually, causing upheaval, dislocation, emotional trauma, pain, division, and general apathy. This has destroyed many families. I and many others were forced into believing in Christianity and at the same time were confronted with sexual abuse. How does one justify the years of pain? Trying to adjust to the European way of thinking confused me emotionally and destroyed my peace of mind with continuous flashbacks.

I still have many Colebrook sisters, but I am deeply saddened by the loss of our brothers. I believe that our brothers were confused and lost and had a sense of hopelessness. So it was all too easy to turn to alcohol to deaden the pain. We know this was not the answer because so many have died at an early age. Can someone tell me what was the answer?

(L–R): Ray Argent and Ronald Guirkin both deceased.

I have been inspired by many events that occurred throughout my life which challenged me to write this book. A lot of truth could be told. In writing this book, I have been fulfilled and healed of all my anguish and disillusion. I think that it's important that my grandchildren should know where their Nanna came from and know about Colebrook Home. It's important that my children and grandchildren know of my hardships and all that I have endured over the years. My pen and paper are my trade.

To help in writing this book I decided to attend college to improve my English and literacy. I had already started on the book on my own at home but I felt isolated. I enrolled at the Torrens Valley Institute of TAFE at Gilles Plains and paid my fees. I was then accepted as one of the students. On my first day, I was met by Don Strempel and my teacher, Una, his wife. I was nervous but Una was most helpful.

I did not have the confidence or the patience. I recall being a seriously angry person, angrily screwing up the pages I had written. 'I will never get this book done!' I said to Una repeatedly. Our first big task was to draw up a plan to use as a guideline. Amazingly, remembering so much of my childhood came quite easily, the good and the bad things.

There were times I was not well. I wandered around the campus thinking that I was on the grounds of an institution. I'm not *cutta* I murmured. I always saw the day through somehow. The staff were always there. I had a good relationship with all the staff members. I attended college and then I had extra assistance from Zora who tutored me one night a week. I nicknamed her 'Zora the Greek'. Zora accepted the humour but her husband calls her 'Zorric'. Poor Zora has put up with my mood swings and my sudden lack of interest in completing this bloody book.

I knew I still had to put pen to paper to make people aware of the traumas that have been inflicted on me in my lifetime and on many Aboriginal children who had suffered by being separated from their families. Going to college has been a learning time and a spiritual healing process both for me and the teachers.

To help me to write this book, I decided to ask a few of my brothers and sisters for their stories. Listening to them has made me feel angry and has brought tears to my eyes. It was very hard for these people to present the sorrows that they had endured for many years. These disturbing stories did happen. We will never forget. The thing is that when we share the pain we begin to heal.

A few years back, my day was made by the arrival of my older Colebrook sister, Joyce, from Darwin. We sat in my kitchen and I pulled out the old biscuit tin to browse through some black and white photographs of the Colebrook children. This was part of my healing. As Joyce shared her memories, we recaptured our experience of Colebrook Home and our memories of two other sisters. Joyce recalled the dormitories being divided and her greatest fear was for the welfare of her two younger brothers. Being protective, she was concerned and repeatedly checked her younger brothers by sneaking around to the boys' dormitory. Joyce remembered cries coming from the boys' dormitories. Years later Joyce learnt that some of the boys had been molested.

Joyce also recalled being punished after stealing butter from the staff room. She had saved her slices of bread to enjoy the taste of butter. The children weren't allowed to have butter. We only used dripping on our bread. We were encouraged to eat all this wonderful starchy food, rice pud-dings and sago and bread and butter puddings. While we were chatting we both remembered and called out in unison, 'Do you remember having this?' We both distinctly remembered having bread and dripping. We added salt to make it bearable.

There were children who were favoured and then there were children who were treated badly. One of my sisters, Catherine Appleton, recalls being ill-treated over the years in Colebrook. Catherine was repeatedly told that she was not liked. A staff member simply said, 'We don't like you.' This had an immense psychological effect on her life in later years. Catherine says she will never forget the way she was treated and the way that the other kids were dealt with. Catherine vividly recalls incidences where young children were physically abused by having their pants pulled down in the open, in the courtyard. Then picked up by their feet with their head dangling down, they were belted across the buttocks.

On visiting one of my older sisters, Bessie, I was horrified to hear the disturbing things she had to say. Bessie recalled that a senior staff member interfered with the boys, frequently sneaking around the boys' dormitories to sexually abuse them. As we sat in her small kitchen, Bessie started to cry and in a trembling voice told me that she remembered everything that happened to her younger brother, Ian. Bessie was woken by the sound of crying. She remembers jumping from her bed and found it was her baby brother who was lying in his cot, wet and alone, screaming his little heart out. Not long after, baby Ian died. On the verge of tears, I sat and listened. All I could hear was Bessie crying and saying repeatedly, 'I remember. I remember. I'm not silly.' I listened and watched with anger as Bessie spoke, stumbling for words, her face expressing great sadness. I felt for her and gave her a hug. There was an understanding between us. Being with Bessie, I suddenly felt a boost of strength. It was a time of healing for both of us as we embraced in the

Back row (L–R): Adeline James (deceased), Joan Giles.
Middle row (L–R): Avis Edwards, Ray Argent (deceased), Billy Forbes, Francis Mchughes (deceased), Dennis Rankine (deceased), Frank Kemp.
Front row (L–R): Douglas Hart, David James.

middle of the kitchen. I came away from Bessie's, feeling angered and repulsed.

I have heard many stories of this sort of thing happening to the boys and I now understand the anguish and frustration that Bessie has carried in silence over the years. Not being able to share this dreadful experience. What has the government got to say and who was responsible? How can it compensate all the Aboriginal children who were taken away and had their life destroyed?

Many of the children went on holidays or had weekends away from the home. I recall one particular boy, the deceased JJ, nicknamed 'Chambers'. He was sent away on a holiday up north. He was simply told, 'You're going away.' He had no choice in the matter. He was just twelve years old. He did not return to Colebrook. Where were the guiding hands? Where can a child turn? What can a child do? He ended up in Birdsville doing a man's job, working as a stockman, earning just two pounds a week. This did not bother JJ, but he did miss his brothers and sisters. At times he became distressed knowing that he would never see them again. He was smart and clever and stayed where he knew he was wanted. The late JJ was a child who was not liked by the staff at Colebrook and never returned home. This also had a great effect on him in later years. He was angry and still had bad memories of Colebrook. I met JJ on numerous occasions when he visited me at my home, knowing that I was in the process of writing this book. JJ told me that he remembered earning seven hundred pounds. Funny thing is that he doesn't recall spending it or actually receiving it. He was not taught to handle money. He never received the guidance. I was distraught to hear what JJ had told me. He said, '*Kungka*,' as he always called me, 'They didn't give a shit about us kids.'

Back row (L–R): Elsa Cooper, Coral James, Pam Hunter, -?, Wendy Waye.
Middle row (L–R): Margaret Apma, -?, Ray Argent (deceased), -?, -?, -?.
Front row (L–R): Alice Millera, Dennis Matthews, -?.
Far right (sitting on wall): Doris Kartinyeri.

We have lost many brothers from the home who have passed away. Attending funerals brings back many memories of our times at Colebrook. We reminisce and sing many songs that were taught to us. Even today there is still a bond with the Colebrook family and the extended families. I was in Colebrook Home with both of my cousins who I regarded as my brothers and they both passed on in their early forties. I have beautiful memories of them in my heart. The tragic events of our brothers' lives has had an enormous effect on special occasions like the Colebrook reunions.

I am bloody angry to think that the majority of Colebrook children who were victims of being stolen from their families, then became victims of humiliation, shame and guilt. David James remembers one of the boys being reprimanded. The boy was made an example in front of an audience, with all the children lined up to observe the punishment. The boy was handed to the police then marched off to the Magill reformatory. The boys at the home were always dealt with severely if they dared to speak back to the Superintendent.

CONNECTIONS

Sitting in my lounge-room one evening under a dim lamp, I was playing tapes and listening to traditional music. I was once again unwell. Catherine and another friend were with me and I had the tape loud. My mind was in rhythm with the music and I became quite erratic in a frenzied manner, singing and moving with the *maru* tape playing. On the edge of my hearing was, 'Come on *kungka*, switch that off!' I was deep in my own thoughts, relishing the language and the culture of the songs. It gave me understanding of our people and I was connecting with my culture.

I have travelled from the south to the centre of Alice Springs, to the far north, to the west and the Kimberleys. I was searching for my people and my inner self for spiritual healing. I can say that these trips were not lonely trips but an experience. Meeting other Aboriginals from other parts of Australia has been important to me.

During my stay in Derby, I made friends with Lucy and her Aboriginal family who I went and visited every day. One night we sat with local Aborigines in a circle in the red dust chatting as they drank their alcohol. Lucy was with me. Later I had tea with her.

It was a hot day as usual. Scones and soup were made. The night was still and clear.

I have met quite a few people, especially a lot of tourists, on my travels. On my journey back to Adelaide I met a nice German girl who was back-packing around Australia and a few of the local Aboriginals. There was a group of Americans who chattered on the bus. The accent was so strong and broad, I had to move seats.

I had the privilege of hosting a group of ladies from the north, one being a healer, in my house. My friend Minna had rung me to tell me the women were in Adelaide. I prepared myself to be healed. One of the ladies sat near the stereo listening to the country music. The children ran through the house to the patio, speaking their language. It was all moving for me. The lady listening to the tape kindly asked me if she could have it. The surrounding atmosphere brought me a bond which was unexplainable.

I was gently taken aside and the healing began. She put her fist under my ribs and pushed and twisted her fist into my diaphragm. No fuss was made. The other ladies sat quietly. The presence was spiritual and powerful. I felt a sigh of relief and the healing was done. *Palya*.

FINDING MY VOICE

In September 1996, I was privileged to be asked to be a guest at a conference in Alice Springs dealing with the subject of the Stolen Generations. I left for Alice Springs on a Tuesday morning flight. At the airport, I met up with twenty other Aboriginal people and two or three representatives from Aboriginal Legal Rights Movement. We were all welcomed by our host, Trevor Bromley from South Australia, then bused to the Red Centre Resort where we stayed for four days. The conference was organised and planned by the states. We all arrived for our first informal barbecue at the Old Bungalow by the Todd River. The opening ceremony was addressed by various guest speakers.

The conference was enormous, and the subject emotional for everyone. Our aims were for social justice because of the Government's removal of Aboriginal children, beginning in the early nineteen hundreds and continuing to the 1970's. This was a phenomenal happening with young babies removed from their mothers' breast. Children were sexually abused, girls and women were raped and used for domestic labour. This is now an extremely sensitive issue. The whole conference was powerful and a time for healing and unity as we comforted one another.

I was inspired by my experience at the conference, and I wasn't alone. It became overwhelming and shocking to hear guest speakers tell stories of their removal from their families. My stay in Alice Springs was brief. It was an eye opening experience, particularly in meeting some of the locals with so many different languages and cultures.

The Aboriginal Studies in the Nineties Conference provided another opportunity for me to represent the Stolen Generations of South Australia. This involved a trip to the PowerHouse Museum in Sydney. It gave me the opportunity to give a small talk on my experiences of Colebrook. I believe the four Colebrook representatives were positive in presenting our stories of 'the lost generation' to others on a national level. Ian Blencowe, who works as a curator at the Adelaide Museum, organised the photographic displays of the Colebrook children. The black and white photographs dating from 1930 to 1969 were also a focus for discussions during the seminar. They had an impact on the conference.

One of the biggest upheavals for us Ngarrindjeri people has been the South Australian Government's 1993 decision to allow developers to build a bridge from Goolwa to Kumarangk (Hindmarsh Island). This is an important area that has affected much Ngarrindjeri women's business. It became an extremely controversial issue which involved many people nationally and became known worldwide. Our community asked for protection under the Heritage Act and over the next five years there was division and anger at Federal reports, a Royal Commission, appeals and protests. All over the existence of women's sacred and secret business! Many people don't give a damn!

The demonstrations, which were constantly flashed on national television, had a huge impact on me. My spirituality and belief was strongly within me as I watched with disbelief. I wanted to support the Ngarrindjeri women but I couldn't because I didn't know how to. Thanks to the Government, I had my heritage taken away from me when they removed me from my family. I didn't receive the history of my people and had awfully little knowledge about my culture and my heritage. Women's business was never passed down to me but I believed this group of women was fighting for what they believed in. I became a victim full of anger and hopelessness.

Since this time, I have learnt from Doreen about my family and some of my cultural heritage. It angers me that it was too late for me to give my support to my people who fought to stop the bridge. But when the developers started to build the bridge, I was there protesting!

THE NGARRINDJERI LAND

The land is looking for restoration.
I respect my land.
I walk with dignity and pride
on this land of ours
on the Ngarrindjeri land.
My heart is where it belongs
on the Ngarrindjeri land.
We need to follow our dreams.

After nearly forty years I was going back to Colebrook with two of my Colebrook sisters and two people of the Blackwood Reconciliation Group. Joyce had come down to my place for a holiday, travelling down from the north. Apart from a holiday I had at her place in Derby I had not seen her for years. The day was hot and the ground dusty. We followed in a row one by one as we put all our strength into returning home. That beautiful building had gone, with all the woodsheds and cellar. My memories were racing as I walked through the dusty paddock. The sadness came as we watched the emptiness. Contact with the earth was still with us. It belonged to us and was part of us. Joyce who was in front of me bent down to reach for a handful of dirt. Clasping it, she thrust it behind her as we walked together around the Colebrook site. To me it was a religious gesture and a respect for the land that we lived on which was our home.

The impetus for this return came because of the dedication of the Blackwood Reconciliation Group which had its beginnings in a study circle initiated by nursing sister Di Dent. In June 1994, Mike Brown and Colin Nankivelle from the group had made arrangements to meet with me at my place and to talk about the plans for the Colebrook site. Mike Brown began planning to organise the first reunion and negotiating with the Mitcham Council on how to proceed with the development of the site. The Blackwood Reconciliation Group approached the Colebrook residents with genuine respect, passion and concern. We decided a few of us would go and have a look at the old place. The block was bare and showed no evidence of my life and the lives of over three hundred children. This time, we knew that we were not walking on land but on *Kaurna*[18] land. When I lived here before I never knew that it was Kaurna land.

Each time I go back to Colebrook I find it very emotional. This was my home for fourteen years. A lot of things happened there, a lot of abuse against the children; sexual abuse, physical abuse. The mental abuse was bad; Bible bashing and brain washing. The strict upbringing confused us and made us vulnerable to the outside world. All of our brothers are gone.

The first barbecue was held at the Colebrook site with two thousand people there. My grandchildren were among those who planted trees that day. The energy was there but, at first, I felt a sense of scepticism. The Blackwood Reconciliation group grew and I became involved and optimistic about the strength and dedication to the redevelopment of Colebrook. The endless barbecues and meetings with the Blackwood Reconciliation Group brought a better understanding. Money was raised at these events. South Australian Arts greatly contributed to the project. There were some mixed feelings and misunderstanding about the process and final outcomes from

---

18 Kaurna: traditional owners of the greater Adelaide area

some Colebrook residents. However working together on further developments on the Colebrook site was shared by all members of the Blackwood Reconciliation Group. There are now monuments on the site representing the experiences of all the people who were at Colebrook.

The monuments are good, but some elders don't agree with the amount of money being spent there. They think the money could be spent on other things: drug rehabilitation, counselling or cottages up there for Aboriginals and young offenders. Or there could have been a bike trail. Auntie Dora felt that the layout of the Colebrook memorial site had no meaning to her, she felt it was cold. But when she returned her memories of Sisters Hyde and Rutter was very real and warm. Being reunited with the Colebrook family, she was able to renew the bond that was part of the Colebrook family. She said, 'The tears and laughter that echoed on that day was a real experience that I will not forget.'

The memorials have touched many hearts. The home site is important to all of us ex-residents and my vision is to have it visited by my grandchildren and great grand-children and non-Aboriginals so they can share the stories. With the beauty of its natural bush, a lot of people will visit the area. I hope to see barbecues, public amenities, and a place for story-telling so future generations of Australians can acknowledge the three hundred children that lived at Colebrook and our experience in the institutional care of the United Aboriginal Mission.

Now there are all these monuments. The first plaque was put on a rock in 1997, in memory of the Colebrook children who lived here between 1943 and 1972.

The second monument is particularly special because it represents the tears that were shed by the parents of the Stolen Generations. It is called the Fountain of Tears. It was unveiled by Dr. Lowitja O'Donoghue on 31 May 1998. A coolamon used to carry babies sits on top of the granite fountain. Water from the coolamon flows over the faces which are sculpted into the fountain. I was one of the adults privileged to have my face on the rock. This took many sittings. The patience and discipline of Mr. Apponyi, who worked endless hours to perfect his art, gave me time to share sadness and laughter, reminiscing about my experiences at Colebrook with the onlookers.

On 30 May 1999, many people gathered for a Journey of Healing. First a plaque was dedicated to both Sisters Hyde and Rutter who had a profound influence, reflecting their devotion to the missionary cause. We called them Sisters even though they were not Catholics. I loved their endearing natures and appreciate their dedication to my welfare. Their religious teachings still ring in my mind. Even now I can get together with my sisters and sing in harmony the hymns we learnt as children.

And then there is 'my rock'. I had been approached by the Reconciliation Group to see if they could put my verse on a rock alongside a photo of many children who had been removed, placed or stolen. Another meeting was called and a man called Rick Martin who did all the inscriptions on the rock was there at the meeting. The photos are like the ones in my living room. Next to the photo my poem is inscribed, which I read out that afternoon. 'We are the stolen children who were taken away, torn from our mothers' breast.' I am pleased it is there to make the non-indigenous people and the younger *Nungas*[19] aware that this did happen.

Then the statue of the Grieving Mother was unveiled by all the Colebrook *tjitji tjuta*[20]. It is in bronze of a grieving woman seated on a rock. It was touching to see the face of the mother, head bowed, gently spilling her hands. A plaque tells Auntie

---

19 Nunga: aboriginal person
20 tjitji tjuta: children

One of the monuments at Colebrook. Doris' face is on the bottom right.

Muriel's story. 'And every morning as the sun came up the whole family wailed. They did this for 32 years until they saw me again. Who can imagine what a mother went through? But you have to learn to forgive.' I wanted to see a greater emphasis on fathers as well as mothers. My father had to go through the experience of losing his baby daughter. This monument had a powerful effect on me and I received strength from Auntie Lowitja as she wrapped her arms around me. The unveiling brought extreme emotions, and tears were shed by many people.

After the unveiling, Auntie Lowitja O'Donoghue, another Colebrook resident Raymond Finn, and the representative of the Mayor of Mitcham led us in a moving and powerful Journey of Healing. The traditional Aboriginal Music Sticks were brought down from Uluru, a song was played and the sticks were passed between the non-indigenous and indigenous people. We circled the memorial following Amitja Levai, NAIDOC Elder of the Year, as she carried the Music Sticks in the coolamon ... bringing the children home.

NGARRINDJERI MIMINI

I am a fifty-four year old Ngarrindjeri *mimini*.[21] I am proud to be a Nunga. The battles and struggles of living in two worlds that I endured throughout my life have proven my aboriginality. I am Doris. I have learnt to love myself. I love myself. I walk with dignity. I've got a lot to offer to my family and friends and that is <u>LOVE</u>!

I believe that my illness resulted from the combination of deception and despair throughout my life. I believe that I am only now coming to terms with all that I endured in the past. The healing has just begun. My illness is recognised and more accepted by the community, my friends and my family. I keep taking my prescription medication as a ritual and my illness is under control.

I was hospitalised in April 2000 for an operation on my feet. The attendance of friends, health workers,

---

21 mimini: woman

GP Home Link, Domiciliary Care and Royal District Nurses all helped me throughout my recuperation. The attention I received made me feel special and made me laugh with my aches and pains.

My sense of self has been enhanced by the many complements that I have received during the process of writing my story. I have noticed that my self-esteem and self-confidence have blossomed. This is a new experience for me as I have not been used to so much support and encouragement during my lifetime. I had lived in silence for many years. I now have the confidence to express my feelings and to speak quite openly about the contents of this book. I have given speeches at various schools and Reconciliation Groups.

I have been blessed with three children and now I am surrounded with thirteen beautiful grandchildren. I am encompassed with many people who love me and care for me. The bond with my family is growing stronger and stronger. It's bloody good that now I can sit with my family and friends and my brothers and sisters around the table, laughing and joking about all the bizarre incidents in my life.

Well, I must be alright then!

I have lived in Adelaide for fourteen years. Today I look through my kitchen window. I appreciate the beauty that I have in my own back yard. I enjoy nature. Nourishing my body with natural things such as good vegies and herbs keeps me healthy. I stare with wonder at the growth of my shrubs.

I put a young seedling in, a gum tree, and it has grown into a strong tree. The roots make it strong. It stands tall, the morning sun gleaming through the small leaves, birds flying in and out of the spindly branches. I have watched it grow. I call it my Colebrook tree. The tree has good vibes. I give it hugs now and again to stay in touch with Mother Earth. It gives me a sense of strength.

My family means a lot to me, Jennadene, John and Tanya. They are the extended Colebrook family and this means a lot to me. My grandchildren are our future. They are my precious little souls. This book is for them.

I would like to conclude with a song written by my son John Packham. He has dedicated this song for all the children that were taken away and put in this place Colebrook Home.

COLEBROOK HOME

Now I can't feel what you feel
but I can understand cause
I'm part of you and this place,
Colebrook Home.

Well my mother she was taken away
when she was born and put here in this place,
Colebrook Home.
Like brothers and sisters they grew up
and they played games like kick the tin and
    knuckle bones,
Colebrook Home.

Now there's generations of lost souls
wondering around trying to find their homes.
Some of them did, most of them not,
they're still out there,
the kids from Colebrook Home

And I can see the look on their face
and the pain in their eyes
when someone mentions this place,
Colebrook Home
and tears roll down when no one's around

from the memories of this place,
Colebrook Home
Now in and out of Christianity
trying to make some sense of what they were
    told.
They suffered abuse
from the hand that was supposed
to show them the way from this place,
Colebrook Home.

Now they're saying
there's only one lost generation
well then who am I
descendent from this place,
Colebrook Home.

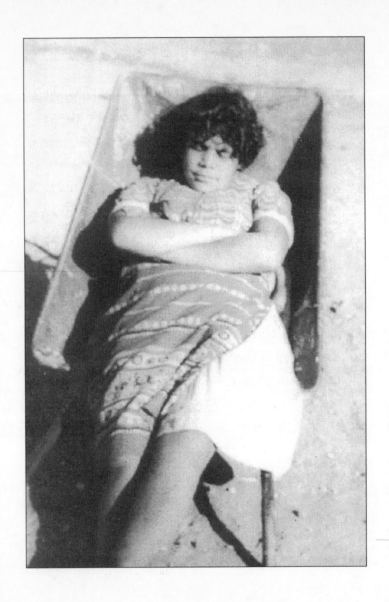